THE PHILOSOPHY OF UPANISHADS

Books by the same author

Dharma : *Man, Religion and Society*

Karma Yoga

Essence of Bhagvad Gita

Atman and Moksha

The Philosophy of Truth

The Hindu Ethics

The Philosophy of
Upanishads

BALBIR SINGH

HUMANITIES PRESS

HUMANITIES PRESS INC
Atlantic Highlands
New Jersey 07716
ISBN 0 391 02935 5

Printed in India.

CONTENTS

PREFACE

The Upanishads occupy a unique position in the philosophical tradition of India. The profound spiritual insights and experiences attained by the Upanishadic seers and sages constitute the basic ingredients of the spiritual heritage of India. When we try to reflect as far back as some three thousand years we can only marvel at the abounding sense of a serious philosophic concern and commitment so conspicuously evidenced in the expositions of these seers and sages. That is perhaps the reason why the Upanishadic philosophy has today come to be recognized as much significant an exposition of human thought as Western or any other philosophy. These seers and sages were philosophers *par excellence*, concerned with explaining all that claimed *to be*, apparently or really.

It was one of the ambitions of the Upanishadic philosophers 'to see life steadily and see it whole'. And this they sought to do not by indulging in unrestrained speculations, but by means of a direct and immediate contact therewith. Their avowed aim was to have a peep into the depths of life itself. Accordingly, in course of time there sprang up various social institutions so designed and developed as to reflect therein the urges and aspirations of the age and provide suitable avenues for their fulfilment. The two such prominent institutions came to be founded on the division of the society into four functional groups (varna), and of life into four stages (ashrama). Consequently, the entire climate in the country was profusely surcharged with a deep spiritual attachment, and the Vedanta tradition of the Upanishads took a definite shape in this process. This was probably the age when the early Greeks were toying with the idea of formulating an ultimate principle of explanation of things, but did not go beyond the conception of a natural cause—such as water, fire, air, etc. But even those who later went beyond such a conception could not discover in them the germ of the matter. The conception of Brahman as the absolute Spirit remains even today unsurpassable in terms of its philosophic profundity and subtlety.

The book purports to be an exposition of the fundamentals of the Upanishadic philosophy, seeking to throw light on the background factors. When thus approached, it became at once clear to me that more important than its superstructure is its foundation so securely and solidly laid by the Upanishadic thinkers in their quest for truth. What has equally weighed with me is the consideration as to how the Upanishads occasioned the rise of the *Gītā* and how they influenced the development of the later Indian thought. If the book could help the reader understand all this in its true perspective I shall deem my labour amply rewarded.

Department of Philosophy,
Hindu College, University of Delhi,
Delhi
6th February, 1983.   Balbir Singh

Chapter I

INTRODUCTORY

That all of us at times are invaded by a recurring sense of discord in the inmost of our being is a self-certifying fact. What an object was a little while ago is not exactly the same now, and what it is now will not remain precisely the same the next moment. Everything helplessly yields to the triple process of origin, development and decay. Man is no exception to this universal law insofar as he participates in the activities of the physical universe. As a natural being he finds himself equipped with a highly developed and organized psycho-physical apparatus designed to facilitate the otherwise mechanical world of matter so as to reach its natural climax in his conscious experience of it. The various organs, sensory and motor, aim at securing an intimate relationship between the psychic and the physical aspects of his being, thereby generating an almost endless chain of action and reaction. This obviously means that both man and the world presuppose and point to each other. If man, on the one hand, is by nature a mere ground of sentient experience, the world, on the other, furnishes the requisite content and thereby makes him a subject, standing over against him as the object. It is this subject-object duality that accounts for all human experience, knowledge and activity. What is agreeable to man appeals to his sentient nature, and what is disagreeable evokes repulsion. In his pursuit of the agreeable he yearns to provide content for the mere form of his sentient nature and hopes to find his good in its enjoyment. He fondly believes that what affords him enjoyment is his good. Since, however, all activity and experience arising from the realm of matter is governed by the iron law of causation, all his pursuits serve only to tighten the grip of natural necessity and bondage on every aspect of his conscious life. In such a mode of his being he is simply one amongst an infinite variety of physical objects and cannot help sub-mitting to the triple process of origin, development and decay. He cannot claim impunity from external determination. So long as he does not awaken to the reality of his own spiritual nature he cannot hope to throw off the yoke of bondage or other-determination.

Indeed, much is presupposed in the develop-ment of that stage whereupon man became conscious of himself as essentially spiritual in nature. It was only in the state of this consciousness that he was able to distinguish himself from all that was merely the blind and mechanical aspect of his being. It is by virtue of this power of consciousness that "man desires to attain the immortal by means of the mortal. Thus is he endowed, while all other creatures are conscious only of hunger and thirst"[1]. This consciousness is the basis of all religious and philosophical developments. It is what has always sustained him in his quest of the immortal.

Consequently, philosophy in India has been traditionally looked upon as a discipline of the highest human concern. The view was widely shared that behind the apparent multiplicity of things of various names and forms (nāma-rūpa) there was the all-inclusive Spirit, called indifferently Brahman, Ātman, Purusha, Chit, etc. All else, then, is but the manifestation of Spirit. In his quest for the truth the primitive Indian was haunted by the recurring question : "Who verily knows and who can here declare where it was born and whence came this creation ?"[2]. What the senses and the mind revealed was only a phenomenal world governed all the time by causes and conditions inherent in its own working. So the ultimate truth could be discovered only by transcending all natural limitations. It was this very question which was persistently asked at the different stages of the development of the Indian tradition in philosophy, thereby paving the way for the evolution of a rich and varied spiritual system. At each stage of this continuous process new ideas emerged, new avenues of reasoning came to be explored and thus gave rise to a huge literature in the form of expositions, treatises, and commentaries. Although, however, the quest at each stage centered around the nature of the ultimate truth, yet the approach was by all means refreshing and reassuring. There arose a bewildering diversity of schools in close succession, and each strove to present its own viewpoint in its own way, occasioning at times a great deal of acrimony.

1. *The Veda : eternal source of knowledge*

The early Indians held the view that Spirit is the absolute truth in the sense that there is nothing else that can consistently claim to be *ultimately* real. The world as revealed in our experience and activity is phenomenal insofar as it is governed by the mechanical law of causation and cannot, therefore, be taken to be the unconditioned reality. It is a mere appearance, a mere shadow apt to be taken as real only by those who are ignorant of the absolute truth of Spirit. Obviously, the pertinent question was : "What is that on knowing which everything else becomes known?"[3]. It must be conceded here that the question cannot be answered by those who can see nothing real beyond the phenomenal world.

It means, then, that the unconditioned and absolute truth of Spirit could be intuited only by those who had experienced it for themselves. It was the truth obtained in an act of direct apprehension on the dawn of which all else melts into nothingness. It is, in other words, "what can be truly seen and entered into"[4], or, as Plotinus aptly put it, "where we stand in the immediate presence of the Infinite, who shines out as from the deeps of the soul"[5]. It is this direct and immediate vision of the Spirit, this act of seeing by means of the soul's inner eye that is the sole concern of philosophy. Hence the name 'darshana' given to it. Assuredly, philosophy in India has definite practical overtones.

Now, the point which the early Indians sought to emphasize was that, while all else was subject to the laws of origin, development and decay, it was the Spirit as such that can alone be accepted as immutable and eternal. While all else has been in a state of change, it is the Spirit alone that has remained self-identical ; it has existed from all eternity and will continue to exist in all eternity. And this means that, if the Spirit has existed from eternity, knowledge thereof has also been available from eternity. From times immemorial such a knowledge has been the object of realization by countless sages. What we call the Veda is the storehouse of such eternal knowledge, and the accredited seers (rishis) are but the media of revelation of this knowledge at the beginning of each aeon. The Veda is but the manifestation of the very spirit of the Ultimate as directly intuited by innumerable sages from eternity and passed on from generation to generation, thereby ensuring continuity of what we call the Vedic tradition. This knowledge has remained unaffected by the passage of time and has ever been available to those who have endeavoured to acquire the vision of the absolute Spirit. It is in this sense that the Veda has claimed to be eternal and impersonal in character. Its authorship cannot be ascribed to man or the gods, since the ultimate truth lies beyond the comprehension of both. Nor can it be conceived as having come into existence during any particular age or era, since the spiritual truth far transcends spatio-temporal limitations. It is, in fact, the embodiment of the eternal Spirit in its actual manifestation through words as traditionally understood by man.

The entire gamut of knowledge is classified into four distinct parts, each associated with the name of a particular Veda : the *Rig-Veda*, composed of hymns to the various deities ; the *Yajur-Veda* which deals with various sacrificial formulas ; the *Sāma-Veda* which contains melodies ; and the *Atharva-Veda* is concerned with spells and incantations. Of these the *Rig-Veda* is believed to be the oldest and is of considerable philosophical significance. In fact, some of the views adumberated in this Hindu text seem to have influenced some of the subsequent developments.

2. *Vedic metaphysics*

Strictly speaking, any *human* attempt to comprehend or understand the nature of the ultimate truth must be utterly inadequate. Human intellect is a tool suited to interpret and explain only the world of our objective experience and activity. The Ultimate is indescribable, and yet we fondly undertake upon ourselves the task of describing it in terms of lifeless concepts and categories. What, then, we can at best say is that it is pure Spirit (purusha) and nothing else besides. "Pure Spirit is all this, all that was, and all that shall be"[6]. It ever abides in its own essence (svadhā), there being nothing beside or besides it to determine and limit it from without. "What is but One, wise people call by different names—as Agni, Yama, and Mātarishvan"[7]. The same view is expressed elsewhere when it is stated that "the worshipful divinity of the gods is but One"[8]. The absolute Spirit is beyond all human modes or ways of description as existent or non-existent (sadasat). Only a being as pure in spirit as the pure Spirit itself could truly know what it is in its inmost core and content. That is why the sages, as pointed out before, have always been looked upon as the significant links in the continuity of Vedic tradition.

The point to be noted here is that the Veda claims to give man the knowledge of a special kind otherwise unattainable by him. It is natural, therefore, that such a knowledge of the ultimate reality must be capable of being interpreted and understood by him. From the human point of view the real, the Veda maintains, is the highest, impersonal law of the spirit that comprehends and

governs the entire universe. It is a law 'necessary'
in its application and 'universal' in its appeal, and
ever abides as the ground of explanation of all that
claims to be, natural and non-natural. Nothing can
claim impunity from the necessary operation of this
law. While it is a law on which a perfectly spiritual
being will act from sheer spontaneity and ease, it is
a law on which a human being *ought* to act, if he is
not so irrational as to be tempted to act otherwise.
Obviously, a man displays complete affinity with
the ultimate truth when he decides to act in conformity with the spirit of this law. But while man
combines in his nature an irrational part and may
or may not act according to the dictates of the law
of his inmost self, natural phenomena do not enjoy
this discretion. Thus, all harmony and purpose so
conspicuously evidenced in Nature is because of the
necessary operation of this law. Whatever happens
here and now has behind it the law of sufficient
reason. There is, therefore, no caprice, no arbitrariness in the working of Nature. All that happens
happens because of the necessity of operation of this
law. The whole universe has followed its own
course since times immemorial, but it has never
outgrown the limits of this law. This is the
celebrated notion of rita which forms the basis of
explanation of the natural as well as the non-natural
phenomena in the universe.

The Vedic philosopher's contention was that
for its unobstructed manifestation rita presupposed
a multiplicity of spiritual beings highest in the scale
of perfection of the spirit of this law. There thus
arose the notion of gods charged with various
cosmic functions and endowed with various

executive powers. All the gods together constitute the unity of the cosmos and are, accordingly, called 'vishve-devas'. As the highest beings in the scale of spiritual perfection, the various deities represent the active manifestation of rita in the maintenance and continuation of the entire cosmic order. No god, however mighty, can transgress the limits circumscribed by rita. All the gods are bound by the inviolable spirit of rita and are, therefore, called the practisers of the unconditioned moral law (ritayu). In their functioning they are all supposed to manifest the spirit of rita and are for this reason called the custodians of rita (ritasya gopā). It is in this sense that they are said to have been born out of rita (ritajāta), to abide by it (ritavan), and flourish in it (ritāvridha). The Vedic gods are, accordingly, to be viewed not only as the embodiments of the moral law but also as the maintainers of the eternal moral order of the universe. They are all supposed to be discharging their respective functions, yet what determines them to act most objectively is the moral law of which they are the custodians. It is the rational necessity of the moral law, then, that accounts for the fact of harmony, purpose, and justice so conspicuously evidenced in every department of Nature. There is, therefore, nothing like indeterminateness, chance or arbitrariness in the working of the entire universe. The whole universe is at bottom a manifestation of absolute rational determination.

When thus conceived as endowed with the spirit of the moral law, the various deities came to be looked upon as the knowers of all our motives and intentions as well as the judge of the moral quality of all our deeds. Prayers were offered to them to forgive sins and lead them to the path of moral rectitude. They are affectionately called 'father', 'mother', 'brother', 'friend', 'comrade' and even 'relative'—expressions indicative of a cordial relation and a sense of deep attachment subsisting between the devotee and the deity. Each deity was supposed to be capable of certain boons as desired by the devotees, and it was but natural that the various gods should be implored to pardon the sins of their devotees and bestow upon them their choicest gifts. The entire universe was conceived as governed by the various deities who had their respective functions and powers. At different stages of the evolution of the Vedic ethos different gods came to be invested with the highest authority and power, thereby implicitly suggesting the notion of a unitary Godhead, called Īshvara.

3. *Vedic ritualism*

The simple faith of the Vedic devotee found its expression in certain outward ceremonies and offerings. In the early stages it was clearly laid down how the various ceremonies would be performed and what ingredients would be used. Since what was of paramount importance was the faith behind the various ceremonies and offerings, external goods to be included in the various offerings were of little consequence. The chief ingredients were generally the melted butter, milk, and grain. The devotee himself could chant the approriate hymns and complete his worship by kindling fire. Sometimes the offerings were made to a particular deity in the hope of begetting sons or possessing other-worldly goods, like cattle, crops ; but sometimes the motive was to propitiate the gods. The sinner could hope to be forgiven by the gods for the sins committed by him. It was widely believed that there are certain kinds of deeds which incur the displeasure and wrath of the gods, while there are others which bring about a closer rapport with the gods, bestowing upon the devotee happiness and prosperity. All such deeds were clearly specified. However, it was the performance of the various ceremonies that was regarded as an important part of the ethical conduct of man.

However, inner faith and purity of heart soon began to be replaced by ceremonial externalism and cumbersome formalities. It came to be fondly believed that the gods granted the boons in propor- tion to the quantum of the goods of sacrifices. The priests were generally invited to officiate at the various ceremonies. They alone would determine how these ceremonies would be performed and what would be required to render them most effective. The entire process of the Vedic ritual came thus to assume new forms. While in the earlier stages the dearest that one could offer to the deities was the whole heart overflowing with faith and devotion, in the succeeding stages the dearest earmarked for sacrifice was some worldly possession, such as wealth, cattle, clothes, etc. Gradually, there arose the cult of animal sacrifice, subsequently supple- mented by the sacrifice of human heads at the altars of the temples. The priests had their own supremacy in almost all the details of the performance of sacrifices. Under the pretext of punctiliousness he would do things in his own way. Naturally, he never failed to take away the lion's share out of the whole sacrifice. The sacrificer dared not question his doings for fear of incurring the wrath of the gods. Thus, the entire Vedic ritual became almost the mockery of those who were of a philosophic temper and could well understand the Vedic metaphysics of the ultimacy of the One—the Supreme Spirit called by different names by different people.

4. *Vedic cosmogony*

From what has preceded in the foregoing pages it must have been abundantly clear to the reader that in the eyes of the Vedic philosopher what alone is real is pure Spirit and *nothing* else besides. In other words, the real is the One (ekam tad), and it is nothing other than pure Consciousness (purusha). The logical corollary to this view is that all else is only of a phenomenal character and is existent only as the basis of explanation by the human intellect in terms of the familiar categories of "being" (sat) and "non-being" (asat). Thus looked at, the Veda, the gods, and the world are only phenomenally real. And this leads irresistibly to the conclusion that they are not as ultimate and absolute as the pure Spirit itself, and that they must have arisen out of the absolute Spirit at some definite point of time. Since they are reflective of the Spirit they cannot be said to be non-existent. They have coexisted from times immemorial. The Veda as the knowledge of the ultimate Spirit was revealed by the sages. The gods cannot be conceived as having been existent by themselves— that is, without the world of whose order they are believed to be the maintainers. And, insofar as they reflect within themselves the exuberant light of the absolute Spirit they are immutable, or, as the Veda itself states, "they are the sons of Immortality." The world arose out of the ultimate Spirit, but none can say when. The process of creation is described in the *Rig-Veda*[9] thus :

At the primeval stage there subsisted only the absolute Spirit, self-complete, without a second. Since nothing else then was existent, it did not lend itself to description in terms of the human categories of "existence." There was nothing else but the pure Spirit abiding in itself—there was no air, no sky, no covering, no water, neither death nor immortality, neither day nor night. The One—the pure Spirit—through an act of self-determination (svadhā) came into being. What had been before in a state of absolute self-subsistence became manifest through the gradual process of self-alienation. The Indeterminable became the determinable through sheer desire of its own. This was the manifestation of mind, the first seed of creation. The One came *to be* through the process of self-negation. The One Spirit came to be particularized as the multiplicity of human souls. The same Spirit gave birth to the world with its innumerable characteristics. The huge mountains, the oceans, the rivers, all came to exist during the process of the alienation of Spirit. But who can after all tell whence this whole universe has arisen ? Assuredly, no gods had been born then. Who else could say anything about the process of creation. It is, therefore, not quite safe to conjecture whether the world came to be carved out by means of the human or the divine hands. Could the Lord in heaven tell us anything about this process ? But there is the doubt whether he was competent enough to describe it as his first-hand experience. This means that the story of creation must ever remain shrouded in mystery. What is simply recorded in the Veda should be taken as the only valid testimony.

Undoubtedly, the account offered here of creation has one great merit. Instead of the account of creation by an external cause, we have here the view that the world is the spontaneous unfolding of the absolute Spirit. And this is taken to mean that the world is only phenomenally real. While from the human point of view it is real, from the ultimate point of view it is unreal, since what alone is real from this point of view is the Spirit. That is why it is often described as the cosmic illusion (māyā). This point received its partial explanation in the Upanishads, as we shall see later. Shankara, the exponent of the doctrine of the ultimacy of Spirit, sought to offer an elaborate explanation of this view. All that meets the eye here and now is but the pure Spirit mistaken for the physical universe.

5. *Transition to Upanishads*

Let us begin by pointing out here that the Veda was basically concerned with providing only the bare outlines of the nature of the ultimate truth. The entire framework within which the deities and the world were fitted pointed to an indescribable reality beyond it. The real could be conceptually interpreted and understood, but not truly known until one had risen to that standpoint from which it was pure Spirit. Indeed, the philosophic insights provided by the Veda were both subtle and profound,

transcending the capacity of the layman to grasp
their true intent and import. Nevertheless, these
insights became the coveted objects of attainment
by those who had the requisite determination. The
need was, therefore, felt to shape a social order that
could be completely congenial for the realization of
tha supreme truth. New ideas took shape, and new
traditions emerged. The entire social order was
oriented to a new direction. The emphasis was on
building a coherent system wherein the individual
could hope to receive the necessary orientation. In
all such planning it was the Vedic spirit that domi-
nated the beliefs and attitudes of the people. The
idea was to orient the entire social order towards
the quest for the ultimate truth as taught in the
Veda. The emerging tradition found its logical
culmination in the Upanishads. The Upanishads
are, accordingly, called the concluding portions of
the Veda (Vedānta)[10]. The philosophic insights
provided by the Veda reach their climax in the
spiritual vision of the Upanishadic sages.

The etymological meaning of the term
'Upanishad' is 'to sit' (sad) 'close by' (upa)
'devotedly' (ni), and is suggestive of the manner in
which the Upanishadic truths were sought to be
taught to the spiritual aspirants who sat around
their teachers in a spirit of devotion. The spiritual
aspirants were expected to live with their teachers
by the time they had grasped the full meaning and
significance of these truths and had mentally and
physically come up to the required standard. These
truths aimed at revealing 'the highest mystery'
(paramam guhyam)[11], and were to be taken without
doubt as constituting the most secret teaching

(guhya-ādesha)[12]. It is in this sense that the truth "Absolute of the absolute" is described as the *upanishad* of the ultimate Spirit (satyasya satyam)[13]. Shankara, a chief commentator on the Upanishads, regards the term 'upanishad' as synonymous with that discipline the pursuit of which culminates in the destruction of all ignorance and the consequent rise of the knowledge of Brahman, the absolute Spirit[14].

All the Upanishads claim to furnish knowledge of the ultimate reality which is otherwise unattainable to man. They embody the rich spiritual experiences of those who sought to attain the highest truth. In the Upanishads we encounter the names of various sages and seers, such as Yājñavalkya, Shvetaketu, Nachiketa, Aruni, Shāndilya, etc. They were perhaps the early exponents of the doctrines attributed to them. In certain Upanishads the truth is sought to be brought out by means of dialogues between the father and the son, husband and the wife, the student and his teacher, and even between the young spiritual aspirant and a certain god. The aim was to arrive at the notion of the ultimate reality through the gradual and systematic exposition of all the relevant details. Obviously, the idea was to remove all doubts and misgivings about the nature of the ultimate truth, so that the aspirant could himself meditate on the truth and strive for its direct attainment.

There are over two hundred Upanishads, though the traditional number is one hundred and eight. Of these, the principal Upanishads are : *Brihadāranyaka, Chhāndogya, Mundaka, Māndūkya, Taittirīya, Katha, Kena, Prashna, Shvetāshvatara,*

Kaushiṭiki, *Isha*, and *Maitrī*. Some of them are concerned, almost exclusively, with the exposition of the nature of the highest reality, called Brahman or Ātman. One wonders at the subtlety and profundity of approach of the Upanishadic philosophers, who were so keen to put forward their spiritual teachings in such a persuasive style. The teachings of the Upanishads deeply influenced the subsequent currents of Hindu thought, and some later philosophers wrote elaborate commentaries on some of the principal Upanishads. The Upanishadic teachings have their special fascination even for a large part of the orthodox Indians.

6. *Main features of Upanishadic thought*

The development of the Upanishadic tradition marks the beginning of hectic philosophic activity. The transition is from a predominantly polytheistic to a severely monotheistic outlook and temper. Almost every Upanishad affords ample evidence of concerted efforts to lay bare the nature of that ultimate reality which is believed to be the true essence of all beings, physical and spiritual. The Vedic philosophy did not give it any name, presumably because no human concept or category could adequately bring out its true nature. It is, in their view, simply the One (Tad Ekam), the pure Consciousness or Spirit (Purusha), indescribable in terms of the familiar categories of being and non-being. It cannot be conceived as having had a beginning, like the gods and the physical universe. At best it can be conceived as ever abiding in its inmost essence (svadhā). All that claims *to be* can ultimately be referred to Spirit or Consciousness as its underlying ground. While all else is subject to decay, pure Consciousness cannot be liable to change of any sort, for what is mutable is matter. It is Spirit alone, then, that can be said to have abided for ever.

It was precisely this philosophical aspect of the teaching of the Veda that became the basis of all subsequent efforts. The Vedic truth was not questioned. It was accepted *in toto*, but only with a view to meditating on it so as to realize it as one's own true essence. The One of the Veda is the Brahman of the Upanishads. Thus, in the Upanishads Brahman comes to be accepted as the only reality that could truly be said to be the object of all spiritual quest. "All this verily is Brahman" is the key-note of the Upanishadic metaphysics. Thus understood, the Upanishads have no plan to reject the metaphysical standpoint of the Veda ; they only seek to carry it to its logical conclusion. How far they succeeded in this task remains to be judged in the following chapters.

What does not, however, fit into the Upanishadic metaphysical framework was the cult of ritualism prevalent and practised in that age. If the object of quest is the universal Self, sacrifices and offerings were too inadequate to take the agent to the accepted goal. All these were generally motivated by some mundane consideration and were, therefore, selfish at bottom. In most cases rites and sacrifices were performed with a view to the attainment of heaven (svarga-prāpti). This, in the eyes of the Upanishadic philosophers, was not the highest goal, for after the enjoyment of the pleasures of a heavenly life the agent had again to take birth in the world of good and evil (sansāra). For the Upanishadic sages nothing short of the complete realization of the soul as in essence Brahman could be the true ideal worthy of attainment. One could find true bliss only when one had truly entered into his own self and seen it with its own eye. Not the worldly pleasures and pursuits, but only a complete vision of the soul could give the aspirant the type of peace and perfection he could enjoy for ever.

The reasons why the Upanishads were dead set against the sacrificial cult of the age is thus clear. In the *Brihadāraṇyaka Upanishad*[15], it is said that one who worships a divinity other than the self is a domestic animal of the gods. The same text teaches that while Yama, the god of death, has his abode in sacrifice, sacrifice has its basis in the fees paid to the priests[16]. The *Muṇḍaka Upanishad*[17] likens the sacrificial acts to unsafe boats, and those who fasten their hopes on their intrinsic-ness are but fools who are always subject to old age and death. Describing the priestly procession taken out on the eve of a sacrifice, the *Chhāndogya Upanishad*[18] mentions about a procession of dogs chanting in sheer mockery : "Om! Let us eat. Om ! Let us drink." Those who believe in the ultimate efficacy of the Vedic ritual are described as themselves blind led by the blind. It is stated that it can lead one as far as the world of Fathers which, however, is a temporary abode for one and from which one must return to earth to follow the cycle of birth and death again[19].

Accordingly, the cult of sacrifice in the prevalent sense comes to be stoutly denounced, but the concept is given a new orientation in keeping with the philosophy propounded in the Upanishads. The *Brihadāraṇyaka Upanishad*[20] speaks of the horse-sacrifice which comes to be allegorically interpreted. The performance of this sacrifice may, it is said, bring even the lordship of the universe, but spiritual greatness could only be attained by renouncing the whole universe which the Upanishad pictures as a horse.

The Upanishadic tradition in its turn developed new norms, new concepts. The spiritual quest was the dominant urge of this tradition. Various institutions came into existence, and all these reflected in them the same universal urge. In the following chapters we propose to take up for consideration all these norms, concepts and institutions.

References

1. Aitreya Āraṇyaka, III. ii. 2.

2. RV., x. 121.

3. Ibid., x. 129.

4. BG., xi. 54.

5. Vaughan, *Hours with the Mystics*, p. 240.

6. RV. x.90. Purusha evedam sarvam yad bhūtam yachchha bhavyam.

7. Ibid., I. 164.46. Ekam sad viprā bahudhā vadanti, Agni, Yama, Mātarishvan.

8. Ibid., iii.55. Mahat devānām asuratvam ekam.

9. Ibid., x.129.

10. Muṇḍ. Up. III. ii.6 ; Sh. Up. vi.22

11. Sh. Up., vi.22.

12. Chh. Up., III. v. 1-2.

13. Brih. Up., II.i.20.

14. This interpretation is to be found in Shankara's introduc-
     tion to Kaṭh. Up., Brihadāraṇyaka Up., Taittirīya Up.,
     and Muṇḍ. Up.

15. I.iv.10.

16. Ibid., III.ix.21.

17. I.ii.7-10.

18. I.xii.

19. Brih. Up., I.v.16 ; vi-ii. 16 ; Chh. Up., v.x.3-7 ; Prashna
     Up., i.9 ; Muṇḍ. Up., I.ii.10.

20. I.i.1.

Chapter II

BRAHMAN : THE ABSOLUTE SPIRIT

An enquiry into the nature of ultimate truth can be the concern of a man who has somehow come to be convinced that the phenomenal around him cannot adequately answer to the needs of the spiritual in him. He hopes to find peace and tranquility of his spirit, but the conditional and the contingent cannot meet the demand of the unconditioned and the eternal in him. By sheer force inherent in it, the spiritual in him seeks to overflow the boundaries artificially erected by the non-spiritual. The invincible passion for truth dominates his entire outlook and determines his attitude to all that affects him as a psycho-physical being. He wants to come face to face with ultimate truth, but he neither knows what its true nature is, nor is there any source or agency that could impart to him the requisite knowledge. The secret command (guhya ādesha) of the Upanishads is : "One must know the truth"[1]. This is precisely what sums up the basic aim of the enquiry the various Upanishads undertook to conduct.

As we have pointed out in the preceding chapter, the ultimate truth is declared to be the absolute Spirit in the sense that nothing else except it can be said to be ultimately real. In other words, what appears to be the world from the lower point of view (aparā vidyā) is *nothing* but the Spirit from the higher point of view (parā vidyā). But the significant thing to note here is that there is nothing dogmatic about this conclusion. The aim is to let the truth itself to dawn upon the seeker through a process of firm grasp and understanding. The knowledge of the ultimate truth, being by nature extremely subtle (paramam guhyam) could be revealed only to those found fully deserving on examination. Equally important to be taken note of here was the authority behind this revelation, While in most cases the authority was one or other of the various Vedic gods—Indra, Yama, or Prajāpati, in some others it was the father seeking to instruct his son, or the husband seeking to enlighten his wife. In those cases where the subject of discussion is believed to be humanly incomprehensible, it is some god believed to be fully competent for imparting such knowledge in virtue of his being the embodiment of the ultimate Spirit. Points of deep philosophical significance emerge gradually during the dialogues. The avowed aim was to impart so much of knowledge of the supreme secret that the spiritual aspirant could easily grasp. The next part thereof would come only when he had amply proved his worth.

1. *The Nachiketa sacrifice*[2]

Once Vājashravasa, desirous of divine grace, performed a sacrificial ceremony which required him to give away all his possessions. Among these were the cows which were useless for any purpose. Dismayed at this niggardliness, Nachiketā, his young son, who knew the religious significance of such acts, thought to himself : "Surely a sacrificer who seeks to make such useless offerings is doomed to utter darkness." Perturbed by this thought, he went up to his father and uttered these words :

"Father, I too belong to thee ; to whom wilt thou give me ?"

For the first time his father did not reply, but when the same question was put to him again and yet again, he replied with a sense of anguish :

"To Death shalt I give thee."

The brave boy was not at all afraid of the apparently unwelcome words of his father.

"Father," he replied, "It's alright so far as I am concerned. Consider how it has been with those that have passed away before, and how it will be with those that are now alive. Like corn a man ripens and falls to the ground ; like corn he springs up again."

Having thus said the boy made his way to the house of Death. But the god of Death, Yama, was not immediately available for an interview, and the young boy had to wait for his turn for three nights. When the god of Death learnt of his arrival from his attendants, he was told thus :

"A beaming young Brāhmin guest hast come to stay for the last three nights. It is but in the fitness of things that a peace-offering is made to him. In the manner of a traditional welcome thou must receive thou guest, for if a householder showed no due hospitality to a Brāhmin, he will swiftly lose all that he hopes to possess—hope and expectation, friendship and joy, sacrifices and good works, sons, cattle, and all else."

The god of Death rushed to greet the Brāhmin guest with the usual courteous words :

"O Brāhmin, I greet thee. Since thou hast stayed in my house for three nights and thou hast not received my hospitality, I grant thou the right to choose three boons for thyself—one for each night."

"O the god of Death," replied Nachiketā, "so let it be. As the first boon I ask that my father be not anxious about me, that his wrath be appeased, and that when I go back to him he recognizes me and welcomes me."

Yama, the god of Death, granted this boon with pleasure.

Thereupon Nachiketā proceeded further. "Heaven is said to be a place where there is no fear of any sort—the fear of growing old, of hunger and thirst, of sorrow ; all those that are there rejoice and feel happy. Thou, O god, knowest the way of the fire sacrifice that leads to heaven. Tell me all about that sacrifice, for I am possessed of the requisite faith. This is my second wish."

The god of Death agreed to grant him his second boon, and, accordingly, taught him the fire-sacrifice and all other subsidiary rites and ceremonies attending it. Nachiketā gave a very good account of his ability to do again all that he had been taught. Yama was highly pleased with him and declared :

"I grant thee an additional boon. Henceforth shall this sacrifice be called the Nachiketā Sacrifice after thy name. Choose now the third wish."

And then Nachiketā pondered over the next move and said :

"When a man is dead, there are two different opinions : some people say he is, while others say he is not. I could know the truth only when you teach me all about it. This is my third wish."

Apparently amazed at the philosophic curiosity of the young boy, Yama said :

"Even the gods were not quite sure what it all meant. This was a mystery even to the gods. Subtle, indeed, is the truth underlying this mystery, not easy to understand. Choose thou some other gift, O Nachiketā."

But the curiosity of Nachiketā grew still more intense, and he quipped :

"Thou sayest, O Yama, that even the gods were once baffled by this mystery, and that it is not easy to understand. Surely there is no more qualified teacher than thou, nor is there any better boon than this to ask for."

Yama sought to test the spiritual strength of the young aspirant and offered to grant him many other attractive goods.

"Ask for sons and grandsons who shall live a hundred years, cattle in large numbers, elephants, gold, and horses. Choose for thyself vast expanses of land and life for thyself as many years as thou wilt. And, if thou canst imagine aught better, choose wealth and long life. O Nachiketā, prosper then on this vast earth. I shall make thee the enjoyer of all thy desires. Whatever desires are difficult to attain in this world of mortals, ask for the satisfaction of all those desires at thy free will. Celestial maidens, beautiful to behold, those that are not meant for mortals—even such rare gifts, along with their bright chariots and musical instruments—will I gift to thee, ever for thy service. But for the mystery beyond the mortal world do not press me. Release me from this."

But Nachiketā would not budge an inch from his stand. "All these gifts," he replied, "endure till the morrow, and the pleasures they afford are only transient in character. All life is brief. Keep thou horses and chariots, no dance and song for me. Wealth, too, cannot afford true satisfaction. How shall he enjoy wealth, O Yama, who once has seen thee ? Only that boon and that alone which I have chosen do I ask for. Having known what is perishable and mortal, how can I subject myself to death and decay. All wealth, long life—in fact, all that you have promised to bestow on me—is full of vanity. Tell me, therefore, about that secret which is not known to men. No other boon shall I ask thee."

Yama was highly pleased with the invincible determination of the young spiritual aspirant and agreed to divulge to him the supreme secret.

In his long discourse Yama explains to Nachiketā the mystery of Self which is declared to be the support of all that claims to exist.

"The truth of the Self," says Yama, "cannot be comprehended when taught by an ignorant man, for opinions regarding it differ from person to person. Subtler than the subtlest is this Self, and beyond all reasoning. Taught by a teacher who knows the Self and Brahman as but one, a man sheds away false notions and attains to the supreme truth."

"Beyond the great self is the unmanifest ; beyond the unmanifest is the Spirit ; beyond the Spirit there is nothing. That is the end, and that is the final goal. The Self, though hidden in all beings, does not shine forth but can be seen by those subtle seers, through their sharp and subtle intelligence.

Just as fire which is one, entering this world becomes varied in shape according to the object it burns, so also the one Self within all beings becomes varied according to the body it comes to be housed in. The one etern alamidst the transient, the conscious, the one amidst many, who grants their desires, to the wise who perceive Him as abiding in the self, to them is eternal peace, to no others. The sun shines not there, nor the moon and the stars, these lightnings shine not. Where, then, could the fire be ? Everything shines only after that shining light. The shining Spirit illumines the whole world".

"Not by speech, not by mind, not by sight can he be apprehended. How can he be grasped except by him who says, "He is."

"He should be apprehended as existent and also in His real nature—in both ways. When He is apprehended as existent, His real nature reveals itself clearly."

2. *Bhrigu's quest for Truth*

The *Tattiriya Upanishad*[3] records an instructive dialogue between Bhrigu and his father, Varuṇa, about the nature of Brahman. Respectfully approaching his father, Bhrigu said, "Sir, teach me Brahman". The father understood how subtle was the nature of that Truth which his son wanted to attain. So, he began by identifying Brahman with matter, life, mind, etc. The conclusion he sought to arrive at was : "That, verily, from whom all beings are born, in whom they live, that into which, when departing, they enter. That seek to know. That is Brahman." What Bhrigu was enjoined upon to do was to bring about a corresponding change in his outlook, as this was possible by performing austerity (tapas). Hence the first lesson which Varuṇa taught to his son was : "Through austerity seek to know Brahman which is austerity."

Accordingly, Bhrigu performed austerity, and he then knew that "Brahman is matter. For, truly beings are born from matter, when born, they live by matter, and on departing they enter into matter." Having known that, he again approached his father, Varuṇa, and said, "Venerable Sir, teach me Brahman." The reply was : "Through austerity seek to know Brahman. Brahman is austerity."

Accordingly, Bhrigu performed austerity, and he then knew that "Brahman is life. For, truly beings are born from life, when born they live by life, and on departing they enter into life." Having known that, he again approached his father, Varuṇa, and said, "Venerable Sir, teach me Brahman." To him his father said, "Through austerity seek to know Brahman. Brahman is austerity." He performed austerity.

He now knew that "Brahman is mind. For, truly beings are born from mind ; when born, they live by mind, and on departing they enter into mind." Having known that, Bhrigu again approached his father, and said, "Venerable Sir, teach me Brahman." To this his reply was : "Through austerity seek to know Brahman. Brahman is austerity." This time again Bhrigu performed austerity.

He knew that "Brahman is consciousness. For, truly beings are born from consciousness ; when born, they live by consciousness and into consciousness on departing they enter." Having known that, Bhrigu again approached his father, and said, "Venerable

Sir, teach me Brahman." To him his father said, "Through austerity seek to know Brahman. Brahman is austerity." Accordingly, Bhrigu performed austerity and he knew that "Brahman is bliss. For, truly beings here are born from bliss ; when born they live by bliss, and into bliss when departing they enter." This is the truth which Bhrigu, taught by his father, attained as in essence that of his own self. He who attains this truth comes to be possessed of all worldly goods such as health, wealth, cattle, glory and fame, besides excellence in the splendour of sacred wisdom.

3. *The two approaches*

Corresponding to the distinction made between the lower and higher forms of knowledge, alluded to before, the Upanishads speak of two distinct lines of approach to the notion of Brahman. From the point of view of lower knowledge, we have the positive notion of Brahman, while from the point of view of higher knowledge we have a negative notion thereof. We shall first be concerned with the standpoint of the lower knowledge.

From this standpoint all that claims to exist here and now is ultimately grounded in Brahman. It is the final cause, the sole source from which all that meets our eye has sprung forth. "As a spider spins out its web by drawing out threads from within itself, as herbs grow on earth, and as the hair grows on the head and the body of a living being, so there arises the universe from the Imperishable"[3]. Nothing can, therefore, be conceived as falling outside of the all-pervasive Spirit. One of the best known descriptions of this aspect of the Upanishadic teaching is to be found in a section of the *Chhāndogya Upanishad*[1], called Shāndilya-vidyā. After defining Brahman as 'tajjalān'—as that (tat) from which arises (ja) the world, re-absorbs (li) it, and supports (an) it—the section proceeds to explain it as "comprehending all activities, all, desires, all odours, all tastes, reaching all, and so self-complete as ever to be speechless and calm." Elsewhere the same point is sought to be emphasized : "This is the truth, as from a blazing fire sparks of like forms issue forth in thousands, even so many forms of beings issue forth from the immutable and they return into it"[5]. "Brahman, verily, is this immortal. In front is Brahman, behind is Brahman, to the right and to the left. It spreads forth below and above. Brahman, indeed, is this universe. It is the supreme"[6]. Another Upanishad[7] seeks to bring out this point thus : "This is the lord of all, this is the knower of all, this is the inner controller, this is the source of all, this is the beginning and the end of beings."

From the standpoint of higher knowledge (parā-vidyā) nothing seems adequate to be a definition of Brahman. The ultimate Spirit, according to the Upanishads, is not the subject over against the object of knowledge. Since all that ultimately exists is the Spirit, there is no duality or distinction of any kind. All is but Spirit presupposed in all our ordinary experience. "You cannot see the seer of seeing ; you cannot hear the hearer of hearing ; you cannot think the thinker of thinking ; you cannot understand the understander of understanding"[8]. Intellect strives to transcend all determination of 'being' and 'non-being', but soon discovers its incompetence to break into the inmost crust of the Transcendent.

"There the eye goes not, speech goes not, nor the mind ; we know not, we understand not how one can teach this"[9]. Since the Spirit cannot be identified with anything else, and is not amenable to determination in terms of the human categories of being and non-being, it can at best be described negatively as 'not this' (neti, neti)[10]. Brahman can be known by one who has known himself as 'he is'. "Not by speech, not by mind, not by sight can he be apprehended. How can he be apprehended except by one who says 'He is' "[11].

The upshot of our discussion is that Brahman is indefinable in any way. The *Brihadāraṇyaka Upanishad*[12] refers to an interesting dialogue between Gārgī, a learned lady, and Yājñavalkya, a renowned philosopher. The point of discussion centres around the nature of that which is beyond the sky, the past, present, and future. Yājñavalkya, tracing it to its penultimate source, declares it to be space (ākāsha). The discussion goes on till Yājñavalkya is able to arrive at the notion of a reality which does not admit of any description or characterization. "That, O Gārgī, the knowers of Brahman call the Imperishable. It is neither gross nor fine, neither short nor long, neither red nor adhesive, without shadow, without darkness, without air, without space, unattached, without taste, without smell, without sight, without ears, without speech, without mind, without light, without breath, without mouth, without form, and without inside and without outside." Lest the description be taken to be as good as 'pure nothing', Yājñavalkya hastens to add immediately that whatever claims to be, is ultimately traceable to the imperishable, transcendent Spirit.

4. *Brahman as Truth, Consciousness and Infinitude*

The contention of the Upanishads is that whatever is taken to be real here and now is in fact the very negation of the ultimate truth. The physical universe is a mere appearance and does not, therefore, stand the test of truth. It is in this sense, then, that Brahman is declared to be the absolute truth (satyasya satyam). Moreover, all physical objects are in their behaviour blind and mechanical. The real, on the contrary, must be of the nature of consciousness, for consciousness alone can be immutable and eternal. And, lastly, Brahman cannot be conceived as limited by any other agency, since what alone can claim to be real and boundless is the Spirit. All this is summed up by the *Taittirīya Upanishad* thus : Brahman is Truth, Consciousness, and the Boundless[13]. The *Brihadāraṇyaka Upanishad* describes Brahman as Consciousness and Bliss (vijñānam ānandam brahma)[14].

But, one might ask, : does all this not amount to characterization of Brahman in human terms ? The reply to this would be that the Upanishads are the embodiments of the utterances of those sages and seers who had themselves realized the ultimate reality and were, therefore, competent to state in their own ways their own experiences. It is in this sense that such utterances have always been looked upon as authentic and worthy of acceptance by those who seek to tread the spiritual path. The truths contained in the Veda were sought to be realized by a multitude of spiritual aspirants of the succeeding ages. The Upanishads are the records of the realizations of such seers, and therefore called Vedānta. The Upanishadic utterances are as authoritative as the Vedic ones.

From the human point of view Brahman is, of course, indescribable. Buddha, as we know, kept silent when he was asked to answer a number of metaphysical questions. In his commentary on the *Vedānta-sūtra*[15], Shankara refers to an Upanishad, no longer extant, which seeks to bring home to us the virtue of silence in such metaphysical discussions. The occasion is the desire on the part of a student., Bāshkali, to elicit from his teacher, Bādhva, a definite answer to his query about the nature of the ultimate Truth. The only reply the teacher thought he could give was by observing silence. On finding his teacher deliberately silent, the student repeated his request. And the teacher had this to say in reply : "I am teaching you, but you do not understand. The self is silence (upashānto'yam ātmā)."

5. *Further development of the notion of Brahman*

The Upanishadic doctrine of Brahman is in fact so original and so self-consistent that certain subsequent currents of Indian thought found it as worthy of acceptance *in toto*. The *Bhagavad-Gītā* sought to raise the fine edifice of its three disciplines of Karma, Bhakti and Jñāna on the metaphysical foundation of the Upanishads. The Mahāyāna school of Buddhism seems to have been highly impressed by the Upanishadic metaphysics of the ultimate reality. The ultimate truth, according to it, is the Spirit which cannot be defined in terms of the familiar categories of thought—such as substance, relation, etc. It is only when one transcends the limitation of viewing the Ultimate in terms of the categories of intellect that one is able to know that the world of his objective activity and experience is a mere

appearance and that the Spirit is absolute in its
reality.

Shankara, a later Indian thinker, seems to be
the most consistent champion of the absolute spiri-
tualism of the Upanishads. He wrote elaborate
commentaries on the principal Upanishads and
sought to vindicate their contention that the ultimate
truth is the Spirit and that the world is a false
appearance. When, according to him, the spiritual
aspirant has attained the highest stage in the process
of spiritual development he comes to know that all
is but Brahman. His well-known conclusion is :
Brahman alone is real, the world is a mere illusion,
and the individual soul is nothing but the very
essence of Brahman. The use of the dialectic is,
indeed, remarkable. If the reader wants to have a
better grounding in the teaching of the Upanishads
he will be well-advised to undertake the study of
Shankara's Advaita-Vedānta.

6. *Conclusion*

It would hardly be an exaggeration to say that
the Upanishadic doctrine of Brahman is unique in
the history of the entire Indian tradition in philosophy. The profundity and subtlety so conspicuously
evidenced in the enunciation of this doctrine are in
fact without a parallel in the idealistic history of
human thought. The mind behind the exposition
irresistibly sways the reader. Even a casual student
cannot fail to discern in this doctrine the unfatho-
mable depth of a spiritual insight which the Upanishadic sages had attained. These insights transcend
the narrow barriers of race and religion, caste and
creed, and are for this reason truly universal in

appeal and application. A curious seeker of truth will easily discover in the Upanishads all that he desires to know about himself and the world around him. Little wonder, then, if rich tributes have been paid to the philosophic ingenuity of the Upanishadic thinkers even by the non-Indians. For instance, Schopenhauer, a renowned German philosopher, has remarked : "In the whole world there is no study so beneficial and so elevating as that of the Upanishads. It has been the solace of my life, it will be the solace of my death."

References

1. Chh. Up., VII. xv. 4.
2. Katha. Up.. I. ı.
3. Muṇḍ. Up., I. i. 7.
4. Chh. Up., III. xiv. 1, Brih. Up., II.i. 20.
5. Muṇḍ. Up., II. i. 1.
6. Ibid., II. ii. 12.
7. Māṇḍ. Up., 6.
8. Brih. Up., II. iv. 2.
9. Kena Up., i. 3 ; Katha Up., vi. 12 ; Taitt. Up., i. 4 ; Muṇḍ. Up., III. i. 8.
10. Brih. Up., IV. ii. 4.
11. Katha Up., II. iii. 12.
12. Brih. Up., III. viii.
13. Taitt. Up., ii. 1.
14. Brih. Up., III. ix. 28.
15. III. ii. 17.

Chapter III

ĀTMAN : SELF

Although in the ultimate analysis Brahman and Self are declared to be essentially the same, yet we propose to take up the study of the later from a certain point of explanation. As we have pointed out in the preceding chapter, from the ultimate point of view Brahman alone is the ultimate reality, self-complete and all-pervasive. The question that arises here is : Where to find an opening in it through which one can gain entry into its inner essence and truth ? The nature of Brahman, being transcendent to all human characterization, can at best signify only a 'hypothetical something', suggesting little direct and immediate intimacy with what man believes to be his inmost being. It was, therefore, deemed proper by certain Upanishadic thinkers to begin the enquiry with 'self' as such and discover its ultimate affinity with the reality. In other words, the aim is to begin the enquiry with the certainty of self which man claims to be his essential nature. It is through the opening of self, then, that certain Upanishads initiate their discussion. Through a systematic exposition of the nature of self the conclusion is reached that Brahman and Self, the objective and the subjective, are but one and the same. What at first appeared to be a mere dogma or an assumption is found to be the very essence of one's own self. It is the self itself that brings with it the certitude of its being one with Brahman. In what follows in this chapter the theme of our enquiry is this self.

1. *Dialogue between father and son*[1]

When Shvetaketu was twelve years old, his father, Uddālaka, said to him, "Shvetaketu, you must now prepare to go to a school. No member of our family, my boy, has been without knowledge about Brahman. It is not enough to be brāhmin only by birth."

Thereafter, Shvetaketu went to a teacher and studied under him for twelve years. Having been imparted all knowledge about the Veda, Shvetaketu returned home, full of pride in what he had learnt from his teacher. His father soon discovered his son's inability to grasp the full significance of all that he claimed to have learnt. One day he said to his son : "Shvetaketu, since you are now so much conceited and believe yourself to be well-versed in all the religious scriptures, did you care to understand the implications of that teaching by which the unhearable becomes heard, the unperceivable becomes perceived, the unknown becomes known ?"

"What is that teaching, sir ?", asked Shvetaketu.

"My dear, just as by knowing one lump of clay, all things made of clay are known, the modification being only in name and arising from speech, while the truth is that it is all just clay ; just as by knowing a nugget of gold all things made of gold are known, the difference being only in name and arising from speech, and the truth being that all are gold—precisely so is that knowledge, knowing which we know all." Shvetaketu told his father that his teachers, being presumably ignorant about this teaching, did not instruct him thus "Venerable sir, please instruct me about this teaching," requested Shvetaketu.

"Alright," said Uddālaka, and continued thus :

"In the beginning all this was Being alone, one only without a second. Some people say that in the beginning all this was Non-being, only without a second. From that Non-being was produced. But how could all this be so ? How could Being be produced from Non-being. On the contrary, my dear, in the beginning all this was Being alone, one only, without a second. He, the One, thought to himself : 'Let me be many ; let me grow forth.' Thus, he out of himself projected the universe. And having projected such a universe out of himself, he entered into every being. All that claims to be has as its self in him alone. He alone is the essence of all beings. "They have Being as their abode, Being as their support. That which is the subtle essence, this whole world has for its self. That is the true ; that is the Self. That art thou, Shvetaketu."

"Venerable sir," said Shvetaketu, "tell me more about this Self."

"Alright," replied the father. And he continued thus :

"Just as bees make honey by gathering juices from flowering plants and trees, and just as these juices reduced to one honey do not know from what flowers they severally come, even so, my boy, all creatures, when merged in the one being, whether in dreamless sleep or in death, know nothing of their past and their present state, because of the ignorance eclipsing the truth—know not that they exist in him and that from him alone they arise. Whatever be the form of these creatures, whether a lion or a tiger, a bear or a worm, a gnat or a fly, all these are but the manifestations of the same being. All these have their essence in him alone. He is the truth, he is the subtle essence of all. He is the Self. And that, O Shvetaketu, THAT ART THOU."

"Please sir, tell me more about the Self," said Shvetaketu. "Alright," replied the father and he continued thus :

"The rivers in the east flow eastward, the rivers in the west flow westward, and all enter into the sea. From sea to sea they pass, the clouds taking them to the sky as vapour and sending them back to earth as rain. And as these rivers, when they merge into the sea, do not know whether they are this or that river, likewise all those creatures named above, when they have come back from Brahman, know not whence they come."

"All these beings find their essence in him alone. He is the truth, he is the subtle essence of all. He is the Self. And that, Shvetaketu, THAT ART THOU."

"Venerable sir, tell me more about this Self," said Shvetaketu. "Alright," replied his father. He continued thus :

"If some one were to strike at the root of this large tree, it would bleed but continue to live. If he were to strike at its stem, it would bleed but continue to live. If he were to strike at the top, it would bleed but continue to live. Pervaded by the living self, this tree stands erect and takes its nourishment, but if the Self were to depart from one of its branches, that branch would wither away ; if it were to depart from a second, it would also wither way ; if it were to depart from a third that would also wither away ; and if it were to depart from the whole tree, the whole tree would wither away. Likewise, my boy, know this : The body dies when the soul leaves it, but the soul suffers no death."

"All that claims to be has its self in him alone. He is the subtle essence of all. He is the Self. And that, O Shvetaketu, THAT ART THOU."

This dialogue between Uddālaka and his son, Shvetaketu, goes on in a similar vein. What is the objective truth of Spirit is sought to be shown as the subjective Spirit in one's inmost existence. The two are in the ultimate analysis one and the same. This is what Shvetaketu realized for himself and he attained immortality, freedom from the realm of good and bad deeds.

2. *Gods and Demons in quest of Self*

The *Chhāndogya Upanishad*[2] seeks to offer another interesting exposition of the notion of self. The aim is to build up the notion of self through what may be called the process of elimination of all that is not-self from the ultimate point of view. The truth is stated thus : "The self which is free from old age, free from grief, free from hunger, free from thirst, whose desire is truth, whose intention is the real— such a self should be sought after, it should be desired to be comprehended. He obtains all worlds and all desires who, having discovered that self, knows it." Thus declared Prajāpati, and both the gods and the demons heard this discourse with a sense of curiosity. They whispered among themselves : "Ah, let us seek after such a self—the self which, when sought, brings all worlds and all desires." Indra was selected from among the gods and Virochana from among the demons, and both

were deputed to seek enlightenment from Prajāpati.
For thirty-two years both lived under him the
disciplined life of a student of sacred knowledge. At
the expiry of this period they believed themselves to
have qualified for receiving instruction about so
abstruse a subject as the nature of Self, and accordingly presented themselves before Prajāpati. He
asked them ; "Desiring what have you lived the
disciplined life of a student under me ?" Both dis-
closed to him the purpose of their mission. Prajāpati's first instruction to them was : "Have a look
at your reflection in a pan of water and then report
back to me what you see therein." They reported
thus : "Just we ourselves are, so we see ourselves
here—well-dressed and refined." "This is the self,"
was the first instruction of Prajāpati. Thereupon,
both Indra and Virochana returned to their respective camps to report back what they had learnt.
The demons rejoiced in their knowledge that body
was itself the self, and that, therefore, with the
improvement of the body followed the improvement
of the self. But Indra did dot take much time to
realize that such an identification of the soul with
body was unjustifiable by any mode of reasoning.
The natural corollary to such an identification, he
thought, would be that the self became blind when
the body was afflicted by blindness, lame when
the body became lame, crippled when the body
became crippled, and was liable to the process of
decay when the body decayed. So, Indra retraced
his steps and explained all his doubts and difficulties
to his teacher. Again, he was asked to lead the life
of a disciplined student for yet another thirty-two
years. At the expiry of this term Prajāpati told him

thus : "That which moves about happily in a dream is the self." While yet on his way to the gods, Indra soon realized the inadequacy of this teaching, and returned to his teacher to wait for another thirty-two years. What he could not understand was how the self could be free from all mental distractions in the present case, though it could well be imagined that it was free from all bodily afflictions. He was again asked to wait for another thirty-two years. At the expiry of this period Prajāpati instructed him thus : "Now, when one is fast asleep, composed, serene, unaffected by dream-consciousness—that is the Self." On reflection this instruction too was seen to be lacking in truth, and Indra rushed back to his teacher with his new doubts. "How can such a self," he asked Prajāpati, "be different from a state of unconsciousness in which one does not know what one is ?" Prajāpati was now fully convinced of the requisite qualification of his student and counselled him patience for five years more. At the end of this period Prajāpati instructed him thus : "O Maghavan, mortal indeed is this body. It is taken over by death. But it is the support of that bodiless, deathless self. Varily, the embodied self is associated with pleasure and pain for one who is associated with a body. He obtains all worlds and all desires who finds the self and realizes it as such."

The *Brihadāraṇyaka Upanishad*³ states the nature of self in much the same way : "This, verily, is his form which is free from craving, free from evils, free from fear. As a man in the embrace of his beloved wife knows nothing without or within, so the man in the embrace of the conscious self knows nothing without or within. That, verily, is his form in which his desire is fulfilled, in which the self is desire, in which he is without desire and free from sorrow."

3. *The Self in bondage*

Although the Upanishads regard the trans-cendent self as the main focus of attention, yet they are equally aware of all those conditions which cause its bondage. The transcendent self as free from all desires and evils comes to be eclipsed by certain external forces that arise from the realm of the not-self. The Upanishads hold that, although both ethics and religion pertain to "a self which in itself does not become better through good work, nor worse through bad work,"[4] and although their significance is temporal, yet on this ground there is hardly any justification for belittling their impor-tance, since both have their claims on man so long as he is what he is and desires to lead his life in accordance with the best norms of human conduct. It is unanimously agreed that, since the self in its true being is absolutely perfect and free, yet under human limitations it becomes conscious of itself through the limitations of the not-self. It is the self in bondage. There are, of course, degrees of human bondage. Some people are almost completely ignorant of the true norms of ethical behaviour and work only for the satisfaction of their natural self, while others are relatively better enlightened and betray some knowledge of what could be truly good for themselves. With their sustained efforts they seek to ascend to the higher stages of spiritual evolution.

The Upanishads have little sympathy with those who are given to sensual pleasures and blindly follow the dictates of their sensuous selves. "Abiding in the midst of ignorance, wise in their own esteem, thinking themselves to be learned, fools afflicted with troubles, go about like blind men, led by one who is himself blind."[5] They resort to the performance of rituals, sacrifices, and ceremonies because they believe that they would thereby make themselves eternally happy. But the Upanishads caution us against the transient nature of such devices and ask us to ensure understanding of the nature of the truth the attainment of which alone could bring about lasting joy (ānanda). The depth of philosophic wisdom far transcends the short-sightedness of ritualistic ethics, and must, therefore, be the sole aim of all human practices.

Man combines in himself two heterogenous elements : the essential self which is ever beyond the realm of good and evil, and is the source and spring of all eternal peace and happiness ; and the sensuous, emotional self which is the agent of deeds motivated by selfish interests. It is the latter which causes human bondage. The essential self has to migrate from one birth to the other because of the inherent potency of it to produce the results of the deeds performed before. The individual thinks that all those actions that promise satisfaction of his ego-self are worthy of pursuit, but such actions cause bondage of the self, for the fitting results have to be experienced by him in his future embodiments. "Two birds," says the *Muṇḍaka Upanishad*[6], "united with the bond of companionship, cling to one and the same tree. Of these two, the one eats the sweet fruit and the other keeps looking on without eating." The *Maitrī Upanishad*[7] elaborates this point in these words :

"There is, indeed, another, different entity,
called the elemental self—he, who affected by the
bright or the dark fruits of action, enters a good or
an evil womb so that his course is downward or upward and he wanders about affected by the pairs of
opposites. And this is its explanation. The five
subtle elements are called by the name 'elements'.
Likewise, the five gross elements are called by the
name 'elements'. Now, the combination of these is
called the body. Now he, indeed, who is said to be in
the body is called the elemental self. Now its immortal
self is like a drop of water on the lotus leaf. This
(elemental self), verily, is affected by Nature's
qualities. Now because of being affected, he gets to
bewilderment ; because of bewilderment he sees not
the blessed Lord who dwells in himself, the cause
of all action. Borne along and defiled by the stream
of qualities, unstable, wavering, bewildered, full of
desires, distracted, he gets to the state of self-love.
Thinking 'I am he,' 'This is mine,' he binds himself
with his self like a bird in a snare. So, being affected
by the fruits of his action, he enters a good or an
evil womb so that his course is downward or upward
and he wanders about, affected by the pair of
opposites. Which one is this ?"

What the Upanishads call 'Nature' is the realm
of objects with countless names and forms. All
such objects are believed to be charcterized by three
qualities : sattva, the quality of purity and ethical
disposition ; rajas, the quality of activity in things :
and tamas, the quality of obscurity and passivity in
things. These three qualities are inextricably linked
up with one another and are present in all things
which we happen to desire as means to the satisfac-

tion of our ego-self. So long as we continue to be affected by these qualties we cannot cast off our bondage. Man is afflicted by different kinds of desires for different kinds of things in the external world. As a psycho-physical being, he seeks to find satisfaction of all these desires. Pleasure, then becomes his sole concern. But this, in the eyes of the Upanishads, is nothing but bondage. Enmeshed by ties of hundereds of desires he continues to work for their satisfaction, knowing little about his essential self whose satisfaction alone could deliver him from the bondage of the realm of good and evil (sansāra). "The small-minded," says the *Katha Upanishad*[8], "run after outward pleasures. They thus entrap themselves into the snare of all-enveloping death. The wise recognizing life eternal, do not seek the stable among things which are unstable here."

4. *Indefinability of Self*

The Upanishadic Self is, indeed, beyond all human comprehension and characterization. As the *Kena Upanishad*[9] pradoxically states, "To whosoever it is not known, to him it is known ; to whomsoever it is known, he does not know. It is not comprehended by those who do not comprehend it." When instinctively we seek to know it our inveterate tendency is to know it as an object of cognition. We all suffer from this human predicament. We seek to reduce it to a definite concept or category and fondly believe that the self is an object of knowledge like any other object. It is in this sense, then, that the self is declared to be not anything (neti, neti). It is not describable in any way whatever. What it is in its inmost essence it cannot be known from a distance.

Yet the Upanishads seek to paint a broad picture of it by describing it as the Being of all beings. It is the Self hidden in all beings. It is in this sense describable, but from the ultimate point of view such a description is inadequate. In the beginning, the Upanishads point out, there was only the Self as such, without a second. It was at that stage that this Self could say, 'I am'. So long as, therefore, one is not able to rise to the highest point of realization one cannot know what one is in the inmost of one's being.

It is now abundantly clear that no human explanation of Brahman or Self can be fully adequate to its intrinsic nature. That is why it is said to be beyond all explanation (neti, neti). Yet an explanation is necessary in the sense that only then could we have an awareness of the transcendent reality and make efforts to bring it within our reach. Almost all the Upanishads point to the intellect's inaccessibility to the true nature of Brahman, yet an understanding is possible only through the exercise of intellect alone. So we have to distinguish carefully between a theoretical understanding of the nature of the absolute Spirit and a practical realization thereof. The latter follows the former.

We quote a passage from the *Brihadāraṇyaka Upanishad*[10] here :

Ushasta Chākrāyaṇa asked Yājñavalkya : "Yājñavalkya, explain to me the nature of Brahman that is immediately present and directly cognized, who is the self in all things." The reply was "This is your self. This is within all things." The question again was : "What is that which is in all things, Yājñavalkya." And the reply was : "He who breathes in with your breathing in is the self of yours, the self which is in all things. He who breathes out with your breathing out is the self of yours, the self which is in all things. He who breathes about with your breathing about is the self which is in all things. He who breathes up with your breathing up is the self of yours, the self which is in all things. He is your self within all things."

The upshot of this discussion seems to be that Brahman may be regarded as describable from the point of view of lower knowledge (aparā-vidyā), while from the point of view of higher knowledge (parā-vidyā) the Ultimate admits of no description whatever. At the transcendent level there is *nothing* but the Self alone, free from all distinctions and qualities. It is the absolute truth about itself, shining in its pristine glory. It is what it is. And that is the end of the matter.

References

1. Chh. Up. VI.
2. Ibid., VIII. vii.
3. IV. iii. 21.
4. Brih. Up., IV. iv. 22.
5. Muṇḍ. Up., I. ii. 8.
6. Ibid., III. i. 1.
7. Maitrī Up., iii. 2.
8. II. i. 2.
9. ii. 3.
10. III. iv. 1.

Chapter IV

NATURE, MAN AND GOD

If what has preceded is accepted as the chief tenor of the philosophy of Upanishads, it follows that what we ordinarily regarded as the world of diversity of 'names and forms' (nāma-rūpa) is false from the ultimate point of view (parā-vidyā). What is absolutely and unconditionally real is the self. As just pure consciousness, it ever abides as the truth behind all appearances. It alone exists without a second. It is eternal and immutable, and, therefore, free from any possibility of change or modification in its natural integrity. All else is a mere passing show. What endures behind the coming-to-be and the passing away of phenomena is pure consciousness, and *nothing* but that.

However, when we climb down from the giddy heights of such an abstruse metaphysics, we find ourselves in a comparatively comfortable position. Here our intellect is the sole tool of explanation of Being and beings as encountered in our day-to-day experience. We seek to account for all beings in terms of the laws of their behaviour. The Upanishads speak of three *forms* of Being—namely, Nature as the physical being ; Man as a partly physical and partly spiritual being ; and God as a perfectly spiritual being. At this level we have a realm of beings which is valid only from the relative standpoint of our intellect (aparā-vidyā). Unable to grasp the nature of the absolute Spirit, we seek to explain it in terms of the concepts and categories of intellect. Accordingly, we have the world of multiplicity of beings which are all unreal from the ultimate standpoint of the Spirit. That is why intellect is accorded only a secondary place in the scheme of the ultimate reality.

Consequently, we are confronted with the difficult task of explaining the realm of beings. Each of the ultimate beings—namely, Nature, Man and God—has a special function assigned to it. The avowed aim is to offer a comprehensive and consistent account of each of these, the purpose being to bring out the underlying unity of the world of our experience. Whatever claims to be from the point of our ordinary experience is shown to be explicable in terms of the law of each, appropriate to its own being. The picture that comes to be thus painted is one of an organic whole in which the various parts make their respective contributions.

1. *The physical universe*

The question which the Upanishadic philosophers set themselves to answer was : If ultimately the real is but Spirit and nothing else, how is the physical universe to be explained ? Admittedly, the two—spirit and matter—are exclusive of each other. Here again we must clearly distinguish between the two standpoints which we have already referred to— namely, the standpoints of lower and higher knowledge (aparā-parā-vidyā). It follows that the question of the origin and reality of the physical universe arises only from the lower standpoint of knowledge, for from the standpoint of the higher knowledge there is just the oneness of Spirit.

Evidently, it is from the standpoint of the lower knowledge that the *Shvetāshvatara Upanishad* proceeds to ask such questions as : "What is the cause ? Whence are we born ? Whereby do we live ? On what are we grounded ? And, who arranges things in such a way that we experience pains and pleasures ?" The *Upanishad* then seeks to find an ultimate principle in terms of which a possible answer to these questions could be given. The various such principles suggested are : time (kāla), automatism (svabhāva), mechanical necessity (niyati), chance (yadrichhā), loose elements (bhūta), the womb (yoni), and the mere individual (purusha). All these principles cannot, either singly or collectively, account for the truth about the universe. They could at best be described as secondary causes. The ultimate all-inclusive cause, according to the *Upanishad*[1], is the autonomous power of God, hidden in his own qualities.

It is, then, from the standpoint of lower knowledge that we ask for the creator of the universe. But we have already stated that, if Brahman is to be accepted as the absolute and unconditioned truth, he cannot obviously be the creator. In fact, there is no creation so far as the standpoint of the higher knowledge is concerned. However, so long as we are what we are, we cannot help asking for an explanation of the universe around us. The Upanishads declare that God is the creator of this universe around us. God is the First Cause and everything owes its existence because of his will.

The *Taittirīya Upanishad*[2] asserts that God is the cause of the origination, sustenance, and destruction of the universe. The two Upanishads—*Īsha* and *Kena*—endeavour to establish the fact of causality in relation to the physical universe. The former begins with the assertion that whatever is here and now is enveloped by God. The purport of the latter is to ask the basic question : By whom (kena) ? By whom has all this been created ? And the answer given is that God is the prime mover of all things.

But one might still ask for clarification of a point : If Brahman is the absolute Spirit and the world at bottom blind and mechanical matter, how can the two be reconciled to each other ? This problem is sought to be resolved in two ways : one, that the world is but a manifestation of an aspect of Brahman ; and two, that the world as revealed to us is a mere false appearance. Let us explain these two points at length. We first take up the former point.

It is contended that, since Brahman as such has been existent from all eternity, the world must have come into existence at one time or other, and that it must have come out of Brahman alone. The *Taittirīya Upanishad*[3] seeks to bring out this point thus : "He desired, 'May I procreate myself !' He performed austerity. Having performed austerity, he created all this, whatever is here and now. Having created it, into it indeed he entered. "In a similar vein the *Chhāndogya Upanishad*[4] declares : "He thought, 'Would that I were many ! Let me procreate myself." It then proceeds to describe the evolution in gradual yet systematic stages of all things in the world. The *Brihadāraṇyaka Upanishad*[5] seeks to explain how the world was at first non-existent, and how later it was made existent whereupon it acquired distinctions of names and forms (nāma-rūpa). Having made the world existent, the Self, in the words of the *Upanishad*, entered it, even to the nail-tips, much the same way as a razor would be hidden in a razor-case, or fire in a fire-holder. The emanation of the world from Brahman is likened to the ejection of the thread from a spider, to the scattering of sparks from fire, to the sprouting of herbs from the earth, and to the spontaneous growth of the hair on the head and body of a living organism. The whole world works in accordance with its own conditions and causes, and does not at all affect God through its imperfections. As the *Kena Upanishad*[6] puts it : "As the sun, the eye of the world, is not sullied by the eternal defects of the eyes, so the one inner Self of all things is not sullied by the imperfections of the world."

It is now abundantly clear that the physical universe is a real manifestation of God, and he sustains it as its inner spirit. All that takes place here and now has behind it the explicit sanction of God. There is thus no arbitrariness, no caprice, no fiat in his functioning. The world exhibits a definite purpose and harmony because it is sustained by the intelligent will of God. He pervades it as its eternal and immutable Spirit. Being grounded in the eternal laws of God, it functions in its own way.

According to the other view, the world is a mere appearance, an illusion perpetuated by our imperfect vision. If what is real is only the Spirit, the world of matter cannot be the reality itself. In order to understand this point we shall here explain the age-old theory of what is called "māyā."

2. *The concept of Māyā*

'Māyā' is one of the key-concepts often employed by the Hindu texts and philosophers in explaining their world-view. It acquired special significance in the philosophical perspective of Shankara, an influential exponent of the thought of the Upanishads in the eighth century A.D. Since then this concept has become part of the philosophic parlance of the Hindus. Let us discuss the main features of this concept here.

Shankara held that there are three distinct and distinguishable levels of experience, each level representing reality from its own point of view. These three levels are : the level of illusory experience, that of ordinary human experience, and that of complete spiritual experience. Let us illustrate our point by means of the common example of rope-and-snake experience.

Suppose there is a rope lying before me and when I pass by it I instinctively mistake it for a snake under cover of darkness. The moment I am convinced that the object before me is a snake I produce responses characteristic of extreme fear and nervousness. And so long as such an experience lasts I continue to display such responses. Suppose on a closer scrutiny of the situation I find myself in, I learn that the object before me is not a snake but a rope. Immediately the emotion of fear disappears and I regain my normal consciousness. In the light of this illustration let us bring out the various implications of such an experience.

In my perception 'This is a snake' there are two distinct elements to be carefully taken note of : namely, the 'this' or the rope, and the object known as a 'snake'. When I misperceived the rope as a snake what happened was that 'snakeness' came to be superimposed on the rope. The point to be clearly noted here is that the rope has been a rope throughout the whole of my experience. It never became a snake, and yet I happened to mistake it for a snake. How, then, do we explain this optic illusion? According to the Hindus, the act of superimposition is purely subjective. Thus, the object perceived as a snake is merely a creation of my mind. In other words, there was no such object as a snake corresponding to my idea of it in the mind.

The Hindus seek to explain their metaphysical point of view by reference to this example. Their contention is that, just as the mind created the snake, even so the mind creates this world out of its forms. So long as we are possessed of a mental mechanism we cannot help employing its various concepts and categories in the creation of a world for our practical needs. We superimpose our own concepts and categories in the creation of a world for our practical needs. We superimpose our own concepts and categories on what is ultimately of the nature of Self. The resultant world thus created is called 'māyā'. In sharp contrast to the highest realm of Self, the phenomenal world is governed by the law of causation. Whatever is here and now must have a condition for its being. There is nothing unconditioned. All else but Self is enmeshed in the inexorable sway of causal necessity. There is no escape from the law of conditional existence, except through the complete realization of the ultimate truth.

Let us pursue the metaphysical implications of our example still further. When I happened to mistake the rope for a snake, my experience was built upon an underlying object, namely, the rope.

This underlying object, the rope, happened to be eclipsed by my wrong perception. But when the normal vision came to be restored, the underlying object, the rope, was clearly perceived in its true form. I, then, perceived it not as a snake but as a rope. The Hindus point out that what is actually Brahman is mistaken for a world of matter. What underlies our perception of the world is the supreme Self, but owing to our imperfect vision it is wrongly perceived as the world. This is cosmic illusion. So long as we are what we are, we cannot help perceiving the supreme Self as the physical universe with the infinite diversity of names and forms (nāma-rūpa). We cannot lay aside our conceptual framework and perceive the truth as it is in itself.

We must also state here the two basic characteristics of māyā. According to Shankara, māyā or ignorance not only conceals the underlying truth, but also makes it appear as something else instead. For instance, māyā not only concealed the true nature of the rope, but also presented it as a snake. It is in this sense that māyā is said to be not only negative in character, but also positive (bhāva-rūpam) in its appearance.

From our brief discussion of the nature of māyā it is evident that so long as we have the instinctive categories and concepts as the media of our perception, we cannot but remain in a state of ignorance about the true object of our quest. It is because of this mode of our cognition that Brahman is perceived as the world of physical entities. We must, therefore, outgrow our natural heritage if we want to have a vision of the truth. The moment

we are able to do so, we transcend the realm of false
or illusory appearance. We can then see Brahman
as Brahman with the direct vision of our soul.

The concept of māyā as explained above is not
met with in its developed form in the Upanishads.
In the *Brihadāranyaka Upanishad*[7] the Vedic idea of
Indra's assuming many māyā forms with a view to
asserting his existence is repeated. In the
Maitrāyaṇīya, Brahman is compared to a wheel of fire,
an analogy that was later used by Gauḍapāda to
bring out the false character of the world. The
conception of the world as a mere false appearance
(māyā), and God as the weilder of it is clearly
accepted in the *Shvetāshvotara Upanishad*[8]. In the
same text it is stated : "By meditating on him, by
uniting with him, by reflecting on him more and
more, there is complete freedom from the world of
false appearance (māyā)."[9]

3. *God*

We shall begin by reminding the reader that
theism is not the basic concern of the Upanishadic
philosophers. Excepting the *Shvetāshvatara Upanishad*
all other Upanishads are almost indifferent to it.
The sole explanation for this fact is that the
Upanishadic thinkers were concerned with the
notion of the transcendent reality from what we have
already referred to as the standpoint of higher
knowledge. We are, therefore, told that all
multiplicity is the product of the standpoint of lower
knowledge. As the *Kaṭha Upanishad*[10] puts it,
"Whoever perceives multiplicity here goes from
death to death. There is also nothing like variety
here. Whoever perceives anything like variety here

goes from death to death". God, soul, and the world sustain themselves only on the standpoint of lower knowledge. So long as, therefore, we remain confined to such a standpoint we canot have a vision of the ultimate truth. We remain within the orbit of the realm of good and evil.

From the standpoint of lower knowledge, then, God (Īshvara) comes to be viewed as the basis of explanation both of the physical and the moral aspects of the universe. In respect of the former, he is its creator, sustainer, and destroyer. The bewildering diversity so conspicuously evidenced in the physical universe is due solely to the diversity of forms God is possessed of. Three such forms are explicitly stated : jñāna or wisdom which guides the divine mind in the governance of the world ; bala or strength which represents the executive aspect of the divine mind ; and kriyā or activity which manifests itself in the eternal creativity of God. This represents the immanent aspect of Godhead. But he is not wholly exhausted in the physical universe, and is, therefore, partly transcendent (parastāt). He does not share the defects and deficiencies of the world because nothing can determine him in any way whatever. The world chooses its own course by means of its own causes and conditions. He is there simply to ensure that things move in strict conformity with their inherent conditions. So, nothing can be a source of determination for the divine will. "He moves and he does not move ; he is far and he is near ; he is within all this, and he is also outside of all this."[11]

As regards the moral sphere, God comes to be looked upon as the supreme judge of the moral quality of all human deeds (karmādhyaksha), the inner self of all beings (sarvabhūtantarātmā), the indweller in the inmost of all creatures (sarvabhūtadhivasas), and the eternal withness of all that happens here and now (sākshin). Nothing falls outside of the divine will and activity. It is only through God's grace that we can attain his status and obtain a glimpse of his greatness[12]. He is the pure form of thought (svachittastham), and, therefore, the motive-force by which his divine wheel is made to turn[13].

4. *The laws of Matter and Spirit*

A 'law' represents the universal tendency of the phenomena of a particular class or kind to behave in a particular way under all conditions. There is no arbitrariness in the uniform pattern of behaviour of these phenomena. If we are to find contradiction in a law, we shall have to say that it holds good at one time and does not hold good at another. Such a law is not a law at all. A law, as we know, must hold good necessarily and unconditionally, whether we like its operation or not. It comprehends objects of a certain definite kind and is manifested in their behaviour. For instance, the law of gravitation states that all things, without any exception, must be attracted by the earth, and that nothing can defy this law so long as it remains what is comprehended by this law. Newton saw only an apple falling to the ground and started thinking as to the nature of the specific law which had determined its behaviour. And he found on reflection that it was the law of gravitation in absolute conformity with which it had no other option than to fall on the

ground.   All laws have their respective spheres of
operation.   The entire universe is characterized by
law-abidingness.   There is nothing lawless.

From the foregoing it is clear that the two
realms of matter and spirit must have their own
laws in terms of which all their phenomena could be
adequately accounted for.   How do the Hindus seek
to explain the laws of both these spheres or realms ?
This is a very significant question and we must
attempt it here in some detail.

From the standpoint of lower knowledge there
are two ultimate realities : Matter and Spirit.   We
encounter these two in the form of physical things
and human souls.   According to the Hindus, these
two realms must have their respective laws if the
world of our experience is not to be a mere delusion.
What are these laws ?

It is maintained in this context that matter by
itself is inert (jaḍa) and cannot, therefore, cause any
activity, motion or movement.   Karma is this law
of activity.   It is by virtue of karma that the realm
of mattter acquires dynamism and the whole
physical universe is ever active in the production of
things of an infinite variety.   The *Gītā* defines karma
as the creative force by which things are brought
into existence.   Since all objects of our experience
are the modes of matter, they all share the universal
law of karma.   It is because of the law of karma that
the entire universe displays orderly behaviour.

Very much the same way all human souls are
conceived as having their own law.   Just as the
realm of matter has its own law of activity, even so
the soul in its universal aspect must have its own
law.   This law is called dharma.   It is the law on

which every rational soul will necessarily act. It is the objective law of essential selfhood, and transcends all subjective limitations such as natural desires and inclinations. It is the law on which I and you—in fact all rational beings—will necessarily act. In its perfect form it is conceived as embodied in the will of God. It is, in the words of the Upanishad, the highest truth beyond which there is no other reality[14]. The whole universe is conceived as governed by dharma, the law of essential selfhood. There is, therefore, no element of chance, caprice or arbitrariness in the working of the universe. As the law of the conscious, intelligent self, dharma invariably determines the behaviour of the otherwise blind and mechanical realm of matter, and thereby ensures complete harmony and justice. It is in this sense that the whole uiniverse is conceived as displaying an orderly behaviour. It is at bottom spiritual. While at the human plane, all activity is determined by the conscious, intelligent self, at the cosmic level the physical universe is determined by the rational will of God.

It is now abundantly clear that karma as the law of activity of physical beings, and dharma as the law of spiritual beings—whether a perfect soul embodied in the being of a saint or that of God— are inextricably bound up with each other. The law of karma as embodied in the working of the blind, mechanical realm of matter requires the guidance and determination of dharma. The two necessarily go together, whether at the human plane or divine plane. God needs karma as much as the physical universe needs dharma. The one without the other is incomplete. The physical universe which displays the law of activity is blind without the law of spiritual determination, while the will, whether that of man or God, is empty without karma which serves as the ground of its determination. The notion of divine incarnation (avatāra) centres around this explanation. In fact, the *Gīā's* conception of God as a karma-yogin is built up on this explanation.

5. *The status of man*

According to the Hindus, the position of man in this universe is *sui generis* in the sense that he combines in himself essentially two heterogeneous elements : matter and spirit. In respect of the former, he is a body-mind complex, a psycho-phyical being with numerous natural urges and emotions. These urges serve as the springs of all activity. One urge replaces the other, and this process continues till the man ceases to exist in his present form. In his natural being he shares the animal life, guided all the time by the instinctive dispositions and inclinations. In respect of the latter, on the other hand, man is very much like God, the embodiment of pure spirit. Thus, man is neither wholly matter nor wholly spirit, but a unique blend of both. But when he acts from sheer force of his instinctive passions, he creates bondage for himself. He fondly believes that his good lies in the satisfaction of his desires and passions. He hankers after sensual enjoyments, yet nothing is adequate enough to bring him complete satisfaction. In this state he remains oblivious of his true spiritual nature, and behaves very much like any natural object. It is his ignorance (ajñāna or

avidyā), and knows nothing of what could truly
afford him peace and satisfaction. Such ignorance
is destructive of all spiritual insights and efficiency
(jñāna-vijñāna nāshanam). All such actions are
invariably productive of bondage. He is mortal
because he has taken to a natural mode of living. He
is destined to die, but to be born again and reap
the consequences of all his past deeds. He remains
bound to the realm of good and evil (sansāra). The
soul has to migrate along with the subtle dispositions
formed by him in his preceding life. These dispositions produce their appropriate effects in the
succeeding birth. So long as, therefore, he remains in
the grip of his natural urges he continues to be born
and to die. The wheel of transmigration continues
to turn endlessly, as it seems.

In respect of his spiritual nature, man is, on
the other hand, essentially different from all other
beings. His spiritual being has its own law and can
find satisfaction in actions that are in keeping with
its true form. So long as, however, a man remains
confined to the satisfaction of his natural desires he
cannot have a comprehensive outlook on life. He
remains lost to himself. It is only when he has risen
to an awareness of himself as both matter and spirit
that there arises an inner moral conflict within
himself. It may not be easy for him to resist the
force of his natural urges, yet he is all the time
aware of something that impels him to act not for
the sake of any material good but solely for its own
satisfaction. The path to spiritual perfection is
indeed beset with hazards, but if the aspirant has the
requisite determination he must subdue his natural
self by the law of his spirit. It may take him many

births to ascend the ladder of spiritual heights, and
when he has cultivated the necessary will-power he
must ultimately succeed. As the Upanishad itself
declares : "Arise, awake, having attained thy boons,
understand. Sharp as the edge of a razor and hard
to cross, difficult to tread is that path, as the sages
declare."[15]

6. *Reality as the organic whole*

From what has been stated above it is amply
evident that from the standpoint of lower knowledge
reality may be conceived as constituted by three
ultimates : God as the pure spirit governed by the
objective and impersonal law of dharma ; the
physical universe as pure matter governed by the
law of karma ; and the human soul which is subject
to the operation of both these laws. If, on the one
hand, we have physical beings of an infinite variety
subject to the law of karma, we have, on the other
hand, spiritual beings subject to the law of dharma.
And, just as every physical being shares the
universal law of karma, even so every human soul
shares the universal law of dharma. God comprehends the two realms of physical and spiritual
beings. He is the supreme Being and controls both
these spheres. "The one God is hidden in all beings,
all-pervading, the inner self of all beings, the
supreme governor of all activities, who dwells in all
beings, the witness, the knower, the only one devoid
of all qualities."[16]

Unlike matter, God is possessed of consciousness
or pure spirit. Unlike the human souls, God is free
from all desires and inclinations. Nothing can,
therefore, move him. It is his own nature as pure

consciousness keeps him immune from all changes in the physical universe. He is ever established in his own consciousness (svachitta-stham). All that takes place in the phenomenal world is of necessity subject to divine sanction. "The sun does not shine there, neither the moon nor the stars, neither these lightnings nor even the fire burns. After him, when he shines, everything shines ; by his light all this is illumined."[17] There was never a time when the universe did not reflect therein this divine light, since divine consciousness ever prevades it. It is in this sense that the world is eternal, and manifests the eternal divine consciousness in it. Nothing lies outside of divine will and its operation. He comprehends all things because he is the creator of the universe.

Man is, then, neither exclusively spirit nor exclusively matter, but a combination of both. He is essentially of the same status as God, but he lacks this divine status insofar as he is possessed of numerous natural urges and inclinations. If he has the requisite power of spiritual determination he can raise himself above his animal ancestory and attain true peace. The whole teaching of the Upanishads centres around this point. Every man must cultivate the requisite power of discrimination (viveka) and so discipline his will that it issues forth in the determination of all activity by dharma. He must ever strive to realize the supreme divine vision. It is in this way that he can free himself from the bondage of the realm of good and evil and discover his affinity with God.

References

1.　Shvet. Up., I.i. 3.
2.　iii. 1.
3.　Ibid., ii. 6.
4.　VI. ii. 3-4.
5.　I. iv. 7.
6.　v. 9-11.
7.　II. v. 19.
8.　iv. 89.
9.　i. 10.
10.　II. i. 10-11.
11.　Īsha Up., 5.
12.　Shvet. Up. iii. 20 ; vi. 21.
13.　Ibid., vi. 1.
14.　I. iv. 14.
15.　Kaṭha Up., I. iii. 14.
16.　Shvet. Up. vi. 11.
17.　Ibid. vi. 14.

Chapter V

THE UPANISHADIC ETHICS

1. *The place for ethics*

It has been often alleged that there is practically little ethics in the Upanishadic thought. Such an allegation is certainly baseless and rests on an inadequate understanding of the main tenor of the Upanishadic tradition. What is worthy of note in the present context is the fact that the shaping of a definite ethical order was as much the concern of the Upanishadic philosophers as the nature of the ultimate truth. They were well aware of the fact that a sound metaphysical theory must be accompanied by, and conform to, a sound ethical practice. And this obviously meant a complete organization of all social institutions, so that they all reflected therein the ultimate goal man was enjoined to attain. Consequently, various institutions came into existence. Every man had his own role to play in relation to such institutions and discover thereby his fitting place. An attempt was made to define and determine these roles. What weighed most in the minds of the Upanishadic thinkers was the view that these institutions encompassed all the different aspects of the human life—viz., social, ethical and spiritual. Thus, every care was taken to ensure that these institutions were quite adequate in meeting the needs of the man as a whole. It was, however, he himself who had to exercise his own choice as to which of these he emphasized as the chief concern of his life.

While, however, the common man was concerned primarily with himself, it was the sages and seers on whom rested the primary responsibility for enunciating the basic framework of the ethical order. They were the torch-bearers and they never faltered in their determination to provide the requisite guidance in the practical affairs of life. But one thing was quite clear to them. The ethical order had to be so devised that it represented a gradual and systematic ascent of man to the discovery of the ultimale truth. The sole test of the effectiveness of this order was that it met, as far as possible, the needs of the common man in his ascent to the various stages of the spiritual life. If, on the one hand, the Upanishadic philosophers undertook upon themselves the responsibility for passing on to the common man his own experiences of the spiritual life, it was, on the other, his primary concern to prepare for him the guideline for an ethical conduct. The matter of the fact is that they alone were regarded as competent and qualified for guiding the common man in his quest for the supreme truth.

In this quest he had to understand not only the nature of this truth but also his own place in the scheme of things. The basic enquiry the primitive Indians made was with regard to man's status in the ultimate setting. The question often asked was : Who am I ? It is only when man develops an awareness of himself as in essence of the very nature of the ultimate truth that he raises such a question. A recurring sense of incompleteness about himself ever haunts him. Consequently, it is in such a state of awareness that he seeks to shake himself free from all that he believes constitutes his bondage. The Upanishadic thinkers evolved a comprehensive scheme of moral life, and believed that one could attain a vision of the supreme truth by adhereing to the norms of such a life. In what follows it shall be our endeavour to outline such norms.

2. *The ethical order*

The Upanishadic thinkers were of the firm view that an ethical order could truly reflect therein the spiritual aim of life if it was so planned as to comprehend the various stages of the growth and development of such an aim. Each stage aimed at preparing the aspirant for a certain training regarded as indispensable to the attainment of the highest goal of life. Each such stage was called an "āshrama". Four such stages were conceived, each having its own distinct sphere and significance in the total scheme of the spiritual life. Let us attempt a brief description of each of these here.

1. The stage called brahmacharya which was to end at the attainment of puberty, say up to the age of twenty-five.

2. The stage called grihastha which was to continue for the next twenty-five years.

3. The stage called vānaprastha which was to continue for the next twenty-five years.

4. And the stage called samnyāsa which was to continue for the remaining part of life.

It is important to note here that each stage was an integral part of the entire scheme of spiritual life. Each aimed at imparting a certain training to the individual, so that he could gradually and systematically ascend to the higher one. The training involved the development of the total personality of the individual. Not even the emotional aspect was ignored. Only a complete person could successfully bring the goal within his reach.

3. *Obligations of the four stages*

In the Upanishadic age formal education was given by competent teachers at places far away from the humdrum of the community life. The teachers were generally those who had themselves renounced worldly attachments and had acquired requisite qualification for preparing the younger generation for facing the various challenges of life. They lived in forests where they developed centres for specialized training and teaching of the Vedas and other allied subjects such as grammar. The students were expected to live under the constant care of their teacher and submit to the rules of the centre. The aim was to develop the emotional, intellectual, and spiritual aspects of the personality of the students. This training was supposed to be preparatory to the subsequent stages of their lives. The best in them was to be developed. And only a qualified teacher could help them in this task. The chief obligations attached to this stage were the following :

(i) to serve one's teacher with full devotion and carry out his instructions ungrudgingly.

(ii) to acquire knowledge of the truths taught in the Upanishads.

(iii) to perform the duties assigned by the teacher, such as the collection of fire-wood from the forests.

(iv) to exercise full control over one's sex-instinct and sublimate it in such a way that it became a potent force to be utilized in the development of a sound body.

(v) to cultivate virtues like endurance, compassion for all living beings, respect for the elders, etc.

(vi) to offer oblations to the fire every morning and say the prescribed prayers along with his other class-mates.

(vii) to develop faith in the spiritual order of the universe.

Let it be clearly noted here that the brahmacharya stage purported to lay the foundation of a truly integrated life and sought to meet the requirement of the three subsequent stages. It aimed at imparting to the student the sort of a perspective that was to ensure success for him in all walks of life. He was supposed to be imbued with all the good things of life. He was expected to be the embodiment of all the auspicious qualities befitting an ideal student of those days. In fact, every teacher wanted to give his student more than what the latter thought he had acquired. He was instructed to be completely free from vices like conceit, greed, treachery, etc.

It was with this requisite preparation that the student entered the next stage of life, called grihastha. He was now free to marry and lead a house-holder's life and carry out the obligations of his particular station in life. But marriage meant far more than what it is apt to suggest to us today. The two persons of the opposite sex entered into a wedlock as companions in the task of furthering the common spiritual interests. Propagation of children was looked upon as only an accidental, not an essential, function of the institution of marriage. That is why not all people married at any stage of their life. The chief obligations of a house-holder are the following :

(i) Performance of the five sacrificial ceremonies regularly. These include : offering sacrifice to all living beings, serving and entertaining all the guests and strangers with pleasure, offering incense to the sacred fire, paying respects to the memory of the dead by observing funeral rites and other subsidiary rites, and finally, studying the various religious and philosophical texts, such as the Vedas.

(ii) to ensure a happy and contented life by propagating children through cohabitation with his wife. This implies that he should be faithful to his wife and lead a life of mutual good will and understanding.

(iii) To offer donations to the various institutions aiming at social good and also take a leading part in all tasks concerned with social reconstruction.

The grihastha stage of life has its own part to play. It is here that the house-holder is allowed to indulge in the two basic values of life, namely, kāma (pleasures of sex and aesthetic taste exhibited in the enjoyment and appreciation of works of art, painting, music, etc.) and artha (pleasures afforded in the enjoyment of wealth, fame, etc.). But the enjoyment of such values was subject to the requirement of the supreme law of duty. Accordingly, one

could indulge in the satisfaction of such values only
to the extent posssible within the limit of dharma.
One is no more than an animal if one indulges in
the gratification of the instincts of sex and acquisition without limits imposed from within one's own
self Dharma is this limit imposed on every human
being by his own rational self. So, every house-
holder is enjoined to work for the satisfaction of his
various organic urges, but only within the limits of
the supreme principle of morality. Only then can
he ensure for himself a happy married life and also
be instrumental in giving his social group stability
and peace. And this obviously means that a house-
holder should rise above petty selfish interests and
work for the betterment of the entire human race.
A verse from Panchatantra reads :

Small souls enquire, belongs this man

To our own class or clan,

But large-hearted men embrace

As brothers all the human race.

The house-holder has, however, to outgrow
the bonds of worldly attachments. After having
led a married life for a span of twenty-five years he
is enjoined to proceed towards the higher goal of
life. The next stage for him is vānaprastha. At this
stage he is enjoined to retire to the forests where he
must empty himself of all old impressions and traces
of the worldly life and fill himself instead with
spiritual ideas. He has to give up all narrow
attachments and cultivate instead new modes of life
conformable to the spiritual ideal of life. The basic
requirement is the development of the ethical
motivation. He must be free from impulses and
passions, desires and inclinations, and all that he

does must be from sheer spirit of disinterestedness. He works for the good of all beings. He seeks to identify himself with the whole world. So long as he is invaded by a recurring sense of 'I' and 'mine' he cannot be said to have advanced any further in the pursuit of his spiritual goal. Thus, there are two basic problems before a vānaprastha : He has to dissociate himself from the old habits formed during the earlier stage of grihastha ; and replace these habits by those that conform to the spiritual ideal. The path is, indeed, beset by numerous formidable difficulties, but if the aspirant has the requisite determination he will sooner or later surmount them. He is ever inspired by the prospect of a blessed future and does all that he possibly can to tide over all obstacles and impediments. The following discipline was laid down for a recluse :

(i) To wear the bark of trees, and let the hair grow.

(ii) To live on the fruits and roots of the trees of the forest.

(iii) To busy himself with calm contemplation and meditation.

The fourth stage, called samnyāsa, marks the consummation of the preceding period. It is in the vānaprastha stage that the spiritual aspirant has to prepare himself for the final victory. The samnyāsin has to renounce everything and enter into the perfection of his soul. All that is non-spiritual in him must be banished root and branch, leaving the soul alone to shine by its own light. During this stage he strives to perceive himself wholly in the life of his self. All that is done by him is done from sheer ease of his spirit. He is one with the whole universe,

The following discipline is recommended for a man of renunciation :

(i) A life of austerity.

(ii) Full of all good qualities befitting an ideal man on earth.

(iii) Full control over all his senses and mind.

(iv) Free from all instincts of acquisition and possession.

(v) A life of complete self-sufficiency.

The Upanishads believe that it is only through the discipline of renunciation that the ideal of realization can truly be attained. But in order to practise this discipline one must be full of zeal and unshakable determination. The path of renunciation is the most difficult to tread upon. That is why much emphasis has been laid on the need for one's preparation to follow it with an invincible spirit. If the spiritual aspirant has undergone the required training in vānaprastha he has every reason to attain his goal.

4. *General duties*

From what has preceded it is now clear that each stage of life has its specific duties the discharging of which is regarded as unconditionally binding on those who happen to belong to their respective spheres. However, there are certain other duties that are common to all members, irrespective of the particular stages they happen to belong to. These general duties may here be enumerated as follows :

Moral uprightness.

Faith in the spiritual order of the universe.

Refraining from injury to living beings.

Doing good to all creatures.

Speaking the truth under all conditions.

Refraining from theft.

Control over sex instinct.

Volitional determination.

Control over anger.

Cleanliness.

Carrying out all those obligations enjoined by the Veda.

Undertaking fast on specific occasions.

It is pointed out that all these duties are of universal import and need to be carried out unconditionally. No one can claim impunity from the bindingness of these duties on any ground whatever. All these are in one way or other contributory to the attainment of the spiritual goal. They all aim at self-purification (chitta-shuddi). It is by degrees that spiritual perfection can be attained. The performance of these duties ensures the emergence of the spirit in degrees, and one who is committed to the performance thereof gradually approaches the highest goal of life.

5. *Conditions of moral life*

Bondage, according to the Upanishads, means the association of the soul with a psycho-physical complex. The *Taittirīya Upanishad*[1] speaks of the five sheaths (koshas) of the soul : viz., the outermost sheath made of food or the physical body (annarasamaya) ; the sheath of vital functions prāṇamaya) : the sheath of mind (manomaya) ; the sheath of intellect (vijnanamaya) ; and, lastly, the sheath of bliss (ānandamaya). In the language of the later Vedānta, the first is called the gross body (sthūla-sharīra) ; the next three constitute the subtle

body (sūkshama-sharīra). The last sheath is called
the causal body (kāraṇa-sharīra) insofar as the soul
continues to be hidden by this sheath and the agent
remains ignorant of its essence or truth. Covered
by these layers, the soul is not truly known in its
essence. It is the empirical self that acts and reacts,
and the individual becomes part of the natural
order of things. It is in this sense that the soul is
said to become the subject of experiences and
enjoyments. The individual comes to identify
himself with a definite mode of life wherein his ego
determines him to act in a certain way. He develops
a multiplicity of faculties, each concerned with a
specific function. The *Kaṭha Upanishad*[2] likens the
soul to the lord of the chariot, the body to the
chariot, the intellect to the charioteer, the mind to
the reins, the senses to the horses, and the sense-
objects to the roads. In the *Phaedrus* myth Plato
made a similar observation. However, the classifica-
tion is highly significant from the ethical point of
view and all its implications need to be worked out
in detail here.

What is to be clearly noted at the outset is the
fact that man combines in himself two heterogeneous elements, sensibility and rational self. Will,
according to the Upanishads, is ethically neutral.
However, it may come to be determined by either
of these two elements. An action is good, or for
that matter moral, if the force behind volitional
determination is the self. If, on the contrary, the
motive behind volitional determination is some
desire or inclination, the action cannot be ranked as
moral in the strict sense of the term. This is what
is implied in the distinction the *Kaṭha Upanishad*[3]

draws between the good and the pleasant : "Different is the good and different, indeed, is the pleasant. These two, with their different aims, involve a man. Of these two it is well for him who takes hold of the good, but he who chooses the pleasant misses his aim. Both the good and the pleasant approach a man. The wise man considers them both and discriminates. The wise man chooses the good in preference to the pleasant. But the confused man, for the sake of worldly life, chooses the pleasant." Desires, we are told, are transient and their satisfaction cannot afford us lasting peace and happiness. It is up to us to decide as to what aim we shall set before ourselves. "One becomes good by good deeds and evil by evil deeds."[4] What degrees of ethical excellence we have attained depends upon how far we have developed a purely ethical motivation. A man is not good just because he has been able to develop a strong power of moral appreciation. True moral goodness comes about only when the power of moral appreciation accords with the power of moral determination. A certain statement in Sanskrit has this to state : "I know what is moral, yet I have no inclination to do it ; I know what is evil, yet I have no inclination to desist from evil-doing." Much of what a man claims to be his ethical personality is shaped by what kind of desire he wishes to fulfill in his life. "As his desire so is his will ; as his will, so is the deed he does. And, whatever deed he does that alone he attains."[5] Since, however, all desires are directed to the attainment of perishable goods, they cannot ensure the kind of good that man can truly attain. All desires are sources of bondage and need, therefore, to be subjected to the one, supreme aim of self-realization.

Although the highest goal consists in self-realization, a virtuous life is indispensable to the attainment of such a state. We are, therefore, asked to be virtuous. "Not he who has not desisted from bad conduct, not he who is not tranquil, not he who is not composed, not he whose mind is turbulent can attain the supreme aim."[6] One has to undergo complete transformation in order to have a vision of himself. The Upanishads lay it in very unambiguous terms : "Cultivate self-control (dāmyatā), Be generous (dātā), and have compassion (dayā)." One need not fear death if one has come to be convinced that the element in him, his soul, is eternal and never dies.

6. *Some misunderstandings*

We have already referred to one of the common misunderstandings that there is practically no ethics within the frontiers of Upanishadic thought. If what has been stated in this chapter is any indication, we should readily grant that the Upanishadic thinkers were keenly alive to the need for a scheme of ethical living. Accordingly, they spelled out the outlines of the 'four stages of life' (āshrama), each having its specific duties. It was in the proper discharge of these duties that one could hope to advance towards the highest goal of life. Each stage was conceived in such a way that it became preparatory to the other. The immediate aim was to make the individual conscious of his infinite nature as a spiritual being, but such a consciousness could not be possible without first making him an ethical being. The various virtues, such as self-control, generosity, compassion, endurance etc., could be a feature of the individual's conduct only if he was convinced that they were expressions of his spiritual nature. Naturally, one who desires to be spiritual must first be ethical in his behaviour. And there is now little doubt that the Upanishadic philosophers did pay adequate attention to this prerequisite of the spiritual life.

We now address ourselves to another objection which is yet another case of misunderstanding about the Upanishadic thought. "The Indian sages, as the Upanishads speak of them," remarks Gough, "seek for participaticn in divine life, not by pure feeling, high thought, and strenuous endeavour, not by unceasing effort to learn the true and do the right, but by the crushing out of every feeling and every thought, by vacuity, apathy, inaction, and ecstasy."[7] These and other objections are but typical of much that might be said in a similar vein. The impression has persisted that since, according to the Upanishads, the aim is self-realization, what is enjoined is repression of all desires and passions. The truth is far from that. The aim is realization of one's own self as what it is in its purity, but it does not follow that this aim can be achieved through repression of one's desires. The fact that the Upanishads recognized the need for a proper outlet of emotional impulses by formulating a separate scheme of life in the form of grihastha is itself an irrefutable evidence that they never believed in the cult of self-mortification. The stress was more on the need for understanding and knowledge than on suppression of one's feelings. It was through an understanding of one's own self and the nature of the ultimate truth that one could gradually advance towards one's goal. What was needed was a discipline of spiritual inwardness, a process through which one could reach one's inmost self by stages of gradual discovery. It was participation in one's spiritual nature. And all this could be brought about through sustained efforts to understand the truth about one's own self. Without inner determination there could be no realization, but all this does not mean mortification of the flesh. Where the emphasis is on knowledge, how can one afford to indulge in self-mortification ?

References

1. Taitt. Up., ii.
2. Kaṭha Up., iii. 3-4.
3. Ibid., I. ii. 1-2..
4. Brih. Up., III. 11. 13.
5. Ibid., IV. iv. 5.
6. Kaṭha. Up., ii. 24.
7. *Philosophy of the Upanishads*, pp. 226-67.

Chapter VI

MOKSHA : SELF-REALIZATION

One of the basic assumptions of the Upanishadic philosophy consists in the belief that what man is in his essential nature transcends what he knows he is. The transcendent element is the soul, the eternal, immutable spiritual principle essentially different from all that is subject to the processes of change, development and decay. It is what ever abides amidst all change and destruction. While the physical universe is by nature blind and mechanical in its functioning and is governed by inexorable sway of causal necessity, the soul is essentially characterized by 'consciousness' (chit) and 'bliss' (ānanda). It pervades the entire universe of being and is, therefore, 'infinite' (anantam). If, then, there is anything worthy of being called the highest good for man it can only be the soul of which he is possessed, but of which he is seldom aware.

Man comes into existence as a result of the association of soul with a particular psycho-physical structure. So long as this association lasts, all his activities and experiences are animated and sustained by this spiritual element in him. Behind all these activities and experiences there persists this eternal spark in him. We may or may not be aware of this spark in us. But even if we are aware of its existence in us, such an awareness is only indirectly. For instance, we say, 'My mind was filled with pleasure', 'I sustained injury in my hand', etc., It is evident from such instances that there is something other than 'mind', 'hand', etc., with which it comes to be associated in order to make such experiences possible. However, human bondage is brought about when the soul comes to be associated with natural desires and passions the satisfaction of which is fondly believed to be the only good. We hope to find in the satisfaction of our desires the kind of the good which can bring about the satisfaction of our natural ego, but that which lies beyond is eclipsed. But the law of the physical universe is that the like produces the like. All experiences and activities motivated by egoistic pleasures involve the agent in the world of good and evil. He subjects himself to a conditioned mode of existence. He renders himself liable to the operation of the law of karma according to which he continues to transmigrate in order to reap the consequences of his past deeds. He is, thus, enmeshed in a causal nexus. The deeds and their natural consequences force him to be subject to the process of transmigration. He is born, but only to die again. All this is, however, because of his ignorance about the truth of his essential nature. And, so long as he continues to be under the force of natural desires, he remains a mere natural agent. He is involved in a vicious circle of which he knows neither the beginning nor the end. He hopes to find his good, but what he actually finds is his bondage. All pleasures, as Buddha said, are at bottom pain.

So, the Upanishads persistently remind us that the true object of our quest is the eternal, immutable, infinite soul. It is in the realization of the soul that one can truly hope to find his supreme good. Such a good alone ever abides, unlike the transient desires and the consequent pleasure resulting from the

satisfaction thereof. It is the eternal state of blessed-
ness that should be the only aim of an intelligent
person. The ignorant will ever hanker after transient
desires and their objects, oblivious of the truth about
themselves.

1. *The two conceptions of reality*

We shall recall here the distinction the Upanishads draw between the higher and the lower
standpoints of knowledge (parā-aparā-vidyā). Corresponding to this distinction we have the distinction
between the absolute Spirit or Brahman, and God
or Īshvara. From the standpoint of Brahman there
is neither the world nor God, for both these exist
only from the lower point of view. That is to say,
in the context of the ultimate truth there is nothing
else but pure Spirit. This is the highest point of
realization. And one who comes to attain the
highest truth knows of no duality.

But from the standpoint of lower knowledge—
that is, the standpoint of a human being—the world
is real as the source and basis of all his knowledge
and activity. There are various kinds of phenomena
that take place in it, but each phenomenon is
governed by a law appropriate to its nature. So,
the world is the ground of the different kinds of
phenomena that unceasingly continue to take place
in accordance with their respective laws. But the
Upanishadic thinkers' contention is that such a world
cannot be said to be its own origin. It is a world
which displays harmony, purpose, and orderliness in
its working, and cannot, therefore, be regarded as
the fortuitous combination of atoms. Such a world,
in their view, is the expression of a perfect mind,

called God. This means that there is behind this phenomenal world an ultimate, spiritual Being who governs this world (bhuvanesha). The laws are eternal and they alone can ensure an eternal world as revealed in our experience and activity. Such a world is the expression of an intelligent Being. In this sense, then, God is the ultimate cause of the world.

But man cannot claim impunity from the operation of the divine laws. All of us perform various kinds of actions and behind them all there is a definite motive—that of desiring their fruit. But we ourselves cannot bring about the desired results of all our actions. We at times do the evil, and yet believe that what we have done is the right. It is also not necessary that our actions produce their fitting results as and when we desire. Actions have their own mechanism, independently of our subjective desires. But the rule is that good actions produce good results, and bad actions, bad results. As we sow, so shall we reap. This is the principle of justice. God, according to the Upanishads, is the ground of justice. He is the supreme judge of the moral quality of all human deeds (karmādhyaksha), as also the rewarder of fitting results (karmaphaladātā). Thus looked at, God pulsates with each activity of the world. In our language, he is immanent in each activity, and guides it from within. He is ever present in our inmost being (antaryāmin), and ever abides as our very self. However, the Upanishads do not look upon such a reality as absolutely final. Both the world and God are in some sense conditioned by each other. The world presupposes God, as much as God presupposes the world. In this sense the two are relative to each other. In contrast, Brahman as the absolute Spirit is the unconditioned, impersonal reality. However, so long as we are what we are, we shall have to accept the reality of both the world and God.

2. *The two conceptions of perfection*

In conformity with their metaphysical standpoint the Upanishadic philosophers put forward two closely allied ideals conceived as the natural culmination of all ethical activity—viz., the absolutistic, effecting oneness or identity with the absolute Spirit or Brahman (brahma-bhūyam)[1] ; and the theistic, the attaining of a living communion with God (Īshvaraprāpti)[2]. Corresponding to these two ways in which the ideal to be attained is conceived, two main springs of ethical activity are recognized. They are, respectively, self-purification (ātma-shuddhi)[3], and the undertaking of all activity as a means to the fulfilment of the will and command of God (Īshvarārtha)[4]. In respect to the former, the soul is looked upon as the very essence of the all-pervading, absolute Spirit, so that in actions determined thereby there is the promise and potency of realizing something that ever persists as at once the good and the condition of all goodness. One very special characteristic of man is that he seeks to comprehend everything in terms of the stereotyped and static notions of intellect, and thereby creates a world of his own subjectivity, conception, and self-love. "In thinking, 'I am he', 'that is mine', he binds himself like a bird in a snare. Hence a person who has the marks of determination, conception, and self-love is bound. He who is the opposite of these

is liberated. Therefore, shake yourself free from
determination, from conception, and from self-love.
This is the path to Brahman in the world"[5]. It is,
then, thought as the basis of all these marks which
actually keeps us bound to the world which in the
ultimate analysis is but a mere appearance, like a
snake where the underlying reality is the rope. The
conclusion is quite evident ; "Let a man cleanse it
by effort". Only then could the consciousness of the
highest emerge as worthy of our efforts. This is the
mark of liberation, the highest of all the mysteries
and thus has it been said, for by the serenity of
thought one destroys deeds, good and bad, with the
serene self abiding in the self, and he enjoys eternal
happiness[6]. What place can thought have in a realm
where there is nothing but pure Spirit ? To this the
reply is given : "It is not understood by those who
seek to understand it". So long as we try to understand the self by means of thought we remain outside
the orbit of truth and look upon it from outside.
The goal lies beyond all distinctions which are valid
only from the standpoint of thought. What we see
as all this is the world. However, this is 'seeing'
through the normal eyes. But when Arjuna saw the
world with the divine vision gifted to him by Lord
Krishna, he saw it as but the manifestation of the
absolute Spirit, or Brahman. The Upanishads, therefore, declare that "All this, verily, is Brahman'
(ātmevedam sarvam iti). "Sporting in the Self,
performing actions, such a man is the greatest of all
knowers of Brahman." Whatever he does, is the
expression of the pure Spirit, and he does not bother
about its rightness or wrongness. All that he does
is necessarily and objectively right. Others may

regard it as bad, but at bottom there is the universal norm of rightness.

In respect to the latter aspect, God is described as the judge of the moral quality of all human deeds, the indwelling spirit, the witness of all our thoughts and deeds, as also the ultimate abode of the universe. Here also, as in the other case, the aim is to give up the ego-sense, so that the thought of arrogating to oneself the agency of the deeds performed may be destroyed root and branch. Both in thought and deed the devotee (bhakta) seeks to live as the medium of the expression of the divine will, and is ever eager for divine mercy and grace (prasāda). The spiritual in us is the law of our actions, and at times it becomes difficult for us to distinguish between the two : the one is the expression of the other in all beings. God is the perfection both of self and dharma, and wise men alone can intuit him in his infinite essence. "By meditating on him, by uniting with him, by reflecting on him more and more, there comes about complete freedom from the world of false appearance (māyā)."[7]

3. *The characteristics of a liberated soul*

The Upanishads offer a fascinating account of the behaviour of a liberated person. Let us briefly describe such characteristics.

We have already pointed out that all moral distinctions, such as right and wrong, good and bad, hold only for ordinary people like us. We often do what we think we ought not to do. And sometimes we do what we think is right, but objectively all this is wrong. It is out of ignorance that we do what actually we ought not to do. And even if we do

what we think we ought to do there is in us a
recurring sense of incompleteness. The sense of
moral obligatoriness ever haunts us. But this is
not the case with a liberated person. He has
transcended the realm of good and evil, and is ever
determined by the objectivity of his inmost self.
Whatever he does is necessarily right. Virtue
becomes a second nature with him. A liberated
person, therefore, has not to bother why "he has
done the right and why he has done the wrong."[8]
All his actions of themselves accord with the
universal principle of morality.

Moreover, a liberated person so completely
empties himself of all natural desires and inclinations that he comes to be wholly possessed of his
spirit in its pristine glory and essence. Whatever he
had desired to realize has already been realized.
Thus, there remains for him nothing else to be
realized. He delights within himself and lacks
nothing else. The natural in him comes to fall
apart and he is now absolutely contented. He does
not hanker after anything, for his whole being
comes to be pervaded by the universal Spirit. All
fetters fall away the moment he stands in the
presence of his true self. Having transcended the
limitations of the realm of not-self, he becomes
"integrated, of fulfilled purpose, and is freed from
all fear."[9] The perfected soul regains what appeared
lost to it during its earthly sojourn, but never to
lose it again. It is now in its own, having nothing
to own or disown. All that it is in its own has come
to be owned by it, once and for all. It ever abides
in its eternal selfhood. Having attained death-
lessness, it persists as ever Brahman. All processes

of transmigration loosen their hold on it.

The emphasis of the Upanishads is undoubtedly on the need to see oneself as in the setting of the ultimate truth. When one is able to see oneself as in truth one finds his vision completely transformed. "This, verily, is his form which is free from craving, free from all evils, free from fear. As a man, when in the embrace of his beloved wife, knows nothing within or without, even so the person when in the embrace of his intelligent self knows nothing within or without. That, verily, is his form in which his desire is fulfilled, in which his very self is his desire, in which he is without desire, free from any sorrow."[10] Nothing perturbs him, since the liberated soul is all pure in himself. "He is not chased by good ; he is not followed by evil, for then he has passed beyond all the sorrows of the heart."[11]

The liberated person perceives the same soul running through all beings. Nothing is, therefore, high and nothing is low in his vision. The same spirit pervades all beings. He rejoices in the welfare of all these beings. So long as he continues to be associated with the mortal frame of the body he leads a life of detachment and enjoys complete freedom from all internal and external constraints. He is the very embodiment of all the truths taught by the Upanishadic Vedānta.

4. *Who am I ?*

The fundamental question before an inquisitive mind is : Who am I ? The answer given by the Upanishads is that man is neither the body, nor the

senses, nor even the mind and the intellect. All
these are mere adventitious attributes. All these are
the products of matter (prakriti). All these are
subject to the laws of matter. Prakriti reaches its
consummation in evolving such subtle elements as
mind and intellect. Beyond them is the soul. It is
from sheer ignorance that a man comes to identify
himself with the psycho-physical mechanism and,
therefore, behaves in subjection to its laws. There
develops in the individual an ego-sense. It is
because of ignorance of the truth that he is under
the sway of his ego. Whatever he does is for the
satisfaction of the ego. There thus comes about the
bondage-state. He moves within the narrow confines
of his ego. This is the natural aspect of his being.
But far above this aspect there is the spiritual being
which comes to be gradually eclipsed by the
continued egoistically determined actions. The
individual does not rise above his animal ancestry
and remains only at the instinctive level of his
existence.

But those who are conscious of their higher
nature do strive for transcending the narrow limits
of their ago. There are millions of people who do
the right because they are convinced that their true
happiness lies in it. They may not be able to
explain the philosophical implications of their
righteous deeds, yet they are righteous by faith.
Nothing can make them falter in their determination.
So, many people live by sheer faith in the intrinsic
goodness of their righteous deeds. The soul lying in
a latent position gradully paves its way only to
emerge at the surface. This process of emergence
is by degrees. One does not become a saint

overnight. The soul ever strives to regain its intrinsic strength and thereby determines the will. The two processes—viz., volitional determination and moral appreciation—proceed *pari passu* with each other. In the initial stage one may not be able to perceive the rightness of a certain course of action, but if he struggles hard to be righteous a time comes when he is able to appreciate the moral worth of all actions, whether his own or those of others. And if he persists amidst all difficulties and distractions, he reaches a state where the power of moral determination corresponds to the power of moral appreciation. What is recognized as objectively right is done unconditionally, there being no other consideration in the agent's mind. It is this state that is recommended to be attained.

Therefore, the Upanishadic emphasis is on the need to 'know thyself.' And when one has been able to know one's self, one comes to be the very essence of the Universal Spirit. Hence the mystery behind the statement made by the *Chhāndogya Upanishad :* Thou art That (Tat tvam asi). In other words, Shvetaketu, as we have pointed before, is advised to know his transcendent self. Ordinarily, one does not know what one is in the setting of ultimate truth. The need is to pierce through the veil of appearance and discover one's self. The various natural dispositions—such as desires and passions—have so much urge and temptation in them that the individual finds himself helpless to think of any other course of action than the one recommended by them. He remains a committed slave to them. And, consequently, he has to experience in his subsequent life the results produced as a result of his indulgence. Under the powerful influence of these natural dispositions he loses his true self. So long as he remains a slave to his dispositions all his behaviour continues to be determined by the laws appropriate to them— namely, pleasure and pain. But what the Upanishads seek to emphasize is the fact that lasting bliss can be found only in the realization of one's true self.

5. *Aids to self-realization*

The Upanishads hold that the disinterested discharge of one's duties of the various stages of life (āshramas) prepares one for the gradual release from the clutches of the world of good and evil (sansāra). One must, therefore, bring about a total transformation within one's inner being. This can be accomplished by the cultivation of the spirit of complete renunciation (vairāgya, tyāga). But renunciation must be enforced through the acquisition of the right sort of knowledge, for it is through knowledge of the nature of the ultimate truth that ignorance can be finally and fully overcome. This knowledge does not consist in making the spiritual aspirant *become* Brahman, for there is no becoming here. What one has to attain is not a new state, but a state of what one has been from all time. It does not consist in transplanting oneself from one state or position into another ; rather it consists in *being* Brahman. This state is to be brought about by having recourse to three chief disciplines. These are :

1. Listening to spiritual discourses (shravaṇa).

2. Reflection upon what one has learnt (manana).

3. Continued meditation upon the ultimate truth (nidhidhyāsana).

The one stage is preparatory to the other. The spiritual aspirant is urged to be steady in his efforts, for there may be many difficulties and distractions at the different stages of the spiritial development. Unless one has emptied oneself completely of all natural allurements and attractions there is no knowledge of one's true self. The moment one has attained such a knowledge all fetters of bondage fall away. It is here that the aspirant is able to proclaim himself as Brahman, the absolute Self. This is the state of immortality. The Upanishads, therefore, recommend a path that can ultimately lead us to this state of immortality.

"From the unreal lead me to the real.

From darkness lead me to light.

From death lead me to immortality."[12]

References

1. Taitt. Up., iii. 1 ; Mund. Up., III. ii. 9, Chh. Up., II. xxiii. 1, Brih. Up., V. iv. 1. Katha Up., II. ii, 9.
2. Mund. Up., III. i. 3.
3. Ibid., III. i. 8-10.
4. Shvet. Up., iv. 4.
5. Maitri up., iv. 30
6. Ibid., iv. 20.
7. Mund. Up., III. i. 4.
8. Taitt. Up., II. i. 1.
9. Chh. Up., VII. xii. 6.
10. Brih. Up., IV. iii. 21.
11. Ibid., III. X. 5.
12. Brih., Up., I. iii. 28.

Chapter VII

THE GĪTĀ AS AN ETHICAL ALTERNATIVE

The *Bhagavadgītā*—or the *Gītā* as it is popularly known—represents a distinct current of thought in the Indian tradition. Its distinctness consists in its propounding a new ethics, not a new metaphysics. It accepts as final the Upanishadic metaphysics of Brahman. The mode of explanation of such a metaphysics does not differ in any way whatever from that of the Upanishads.[1] Hence in this chapter we leave out of account the metaphysical teaching of the *Gītā*.

As we know, the one dominant feature of the Upanishadic ethics is its almost exclusive emphasis on renunciation. Illustrative of such a renunciation is a verse from the *Muṇḍaka Upanishad*[2] which states thus : "Those who practise penance and faith in the forest, the tranquil knowers who live as mendicants, depart freed from sin through the door of the sun to where dwells the immortal, imperishable Spirit." There was the general impression in the Upanishadic era that karma (activity) was a potent source of human bondage, and needed, therefore, to be given up. Since the early times of the Vedic practice karma meant the various sacrificial rites performed with a view to the propitiation of the various deities. In contrast to the Upanishadic practice of renunciation, the Vedic practice of Karma (karma-kāṇḍa) allowed the agent full indulgence in worldly pleasures and comforts. Thus, there arose two distinct disciplines of activity : that of renunciation (nivritti-mārga), and that of positive participation in the ongoings of the world (pravritti-mārga). The former recognized renunciation of karma as an infallible aid to self-realization, while the latter, on the other hand, preached the necessity of karma in human life and recognized its fruit as a logical consequence. In other words, the one recognized knowledge as the surest means to perfection, while the other accepted karma as a means to a happy rapport between the agent and the deities here, and to the attainment of happiness hereafter. In themselves both represent only partial truths. Karma, if restricted to worldly pleasures and pursuits, lacked the spirit of renunciation, while the spirit of renunciation, if restricted to knowledge, could not reach its natural consummation in self-realization. But both these attitudes, when welded together in a new fashion, could give a new perspective, a new orientation. They would, then, not look contrary but would be complementary to, each other. This was precisely the task for the accomplishment of which the *Gītā* appeared on the scene, but preferred to be identified as no other then an extension of the Upanishadic tradition, thereby claiming for itself the coveted title of an Upanishad, as indicated in each of its eighteen colophons (Bhagavadgītāsu-upanishatsu). Its concern is not with the metaphysics of Brahman (Brahma-vidyā), but with an ethics based upon such a metaphysics (yoga-shāstra).

It will be seen from what follows in the subsequent sections of this chapter that the *Gītā* does not raise any banner of revolt against what in its view could be called the onesided approach of the Upanishads.

Rather, it purports to find an alternative on the ethical front. The ethics of the four-stages of life (āshrama) has no relevance in the new perspective of the *Gītā*. That explains why in all its eighteen chapters there is no mention of such an ethics. The older order changes, yielding place to new. This new order is propounded in detail by the *Gītā*. This gives this Hindu text a unique place in the ethical thought of India.

1. *A new ethical order*

In an earlier chapter we have explained the ethical order that was prevalent during the Upanishadic age. The one peculiar thing about this order was that it was directed towards the *individual* good defined in terms of the realization of one's true self. All the four stages of life were in one way or other concerned with preparing oneself for this good. The first two stages—brahmacharya and grihastha—were conceived as preparatory to the other two later stages of vānaprastha and samnyāsa. Even these two later stages were regarded as directly conducive to the highest good—namely, self-realization.

The *Gītā* does not accept this scheme. The fact is that nowhere in the entire *Gītā* do we encounter even a remote reference to it. Instead it propounds another scheme the details of which are given below.

The fundamental characteristic of the new ethical order is that it is based on the concept of the social, and not of the individual, good. The highest goal is, no doubt, self-realization, as in the Upanishads, but it is regarded as possible of attainment through the performance of one's duty as conducive to the establishing of a sound ethical order. And this means, in other words, total rejection of the Upanishadic order based on the notion of the individual good. And with this goes the older notion of society.

In the new order we have instead the four functional groups distinguishable from one another on the basis of the duties assigned to each. These four groups together with their respective duties are :

I. Brāhmin. He was the highest in the new order. His important duties included the study and teaching of all religious scriptures, performance of the various sacrificial rites on behalf of others, accepting gifts, and providing an intellectual leadership.

II. Kshatriya. He was expected to discharge all functions concerning the internal and external security of the society, give charity, study certain religious scriptures under the guidance of brāhmins, protect the weak and chastise the wicked.

III. Vaishya. All functions concerning agricultural operations, animal husbandry, trade and commerce were assigned to this group.

IV. Shūdra. He was supposed to look after all others. He was required to serve others, especially in those spheres which lay outside the purview of the other three classes.

Obviously, all the four groups were devised on the basis of specialization of functions. According to this division, every member of the society had a definite station of life and certain duties devolved upon each, the performance of which in a spirit of disinterestedness was regarded as morally binding on him. It was in this way that the good of the entire society was sought to be ensured. The aim was to give the entire society a sound basis (loka-sangraha). The good of the individual lay in working for the welfare of all the sentient beings (sarvabhūta-hitam). He could not claim to have his good apart from the social good. What was important for him was to recognize his particular station of life and perform the duties relative thereto, without any hope of recompense.

2. *The occasion for Gītā's teaching*

The *Gītā* forms part of Bhīshma-parva of the *Mahābhārata*, a great Hindu epic. In respect of its metaphysical teaching it is to be regarded as an Upanishad. Accordingly, Brahman is the only reality and the world is but an illusion (māyā). The human soul is but a flame of the divine fire. It is because of the psycho-physical organism that every man regards himself as different from all others. But in respect of his soul he is ultimately of the essence of the absolute Consciousness or Brahman.

However, the occasion for the rise of the *Gītā* is attributed to a story. Kauravas and Pāṇḍavas belong to the same clan and are descendants of a royal family. Duryodhana, who belongs to the former clan, wants to usurp the entire kingdom. The Pāṇḍavas are eventually outwitted and they have to quit the kingdom for undergoing a strenuous exile for fourteen years. Every attempt is made to have them destroyed even during this period of extreme distress and agony. On completing the exile term the Pāndavas return to the capital and seek the restoration of their share of power. But the rival party does not agree to part with even an inch of the territory under their control. The dispute was then to be settled through a battle between the two sides. Arjuna, a Pāndava, comes to the battlefield in a chariot driven by Krishna, the divine incarnate. The venue of the battlefield is Kurukshetra. When Arjuna comes to the battlefield he refuses to fight and throws away his bow, Gāndīva. He is an Kshatriya, a member of the martial race which, as we have noted before, was known for fighting the enemy and keeping the state free from all external and internal dangers. Under the influence of a passion he refuses to fight. His various relatives and friends, even his teacher and elders, are arrayed against his own men. But he does not want to kill them. He himself wants to be slain by his opponents, and even gets ready to take to a life of renunciation.

Avowedly, the basic theme of the *Gītā* is ethical. Arjuna typifies a human being who has to act with either of the two motives : that of duty and inclination. Under the domineering influence of a sensuous, emotional impulse he is not prepared to do his duty. He forgets then that he is the member of a certain class and has, accordingly, to discharge the duties that devolve upon him as a result of his belonging to that class. The power of moral appreciation abandons him for a while and he is, therefore, not able to discriminate between what he ought and what he ought not to do. Under the blinding influence of a passion he was prepared to

do what he ought not to. His moral self had come
to be eclipsed for a while. He often talked of
vairāga (detachment), but the force behind came
from rāga (attachment). And so long as he
remained under the influence of the passion he
could not perceive his dharma. This is the situation
in which most of us find ourselves, and the *Gītā's*
teaching claims to be of universal import precisely
for this reason. It insists upon every man to listen
to the voice of his moral self and do only that which
is dictated by it. Desires and inclinations are not
parts of our spiritual nature and can, therefore,
cause only bondage. We all have a law of our inmost
self, and an action can claim to be truly spiritual
only when the motive behind it comes from it.

3. *The ethical alternative : Karma-yoga*

The entire world, according to the *Gītā*, throbs
with activity. Different kinds of activity present
themselves before man and he has to choose which
of these is worth his efforts. Whatever promises to
satisfy him is chosen, and whatever does not is
rejected. This process continues for the whole of
our lives. What the *Gītā* seeks to emphasize is the
need to understand the mystery of action which in
its view is extremely subtle,[3] baffling the understanding even of the wise men.[4] Unless we properly
understand the true significance of action in human
life we cannot have a happy and peaceful life.

The *Gītā* tells us that the entire world is swept
by the law of activity (karma). Nothing in the
world can claim impunity from the operation of this
universal law. This is equally true of man as a
psycho-physical being. Therefore, says the *Gītā*,

"no one can ever afford to remain without engaging himself in work even for a moment. Every one is made to act helplessly by the modes of Nature."[5] Nay, even the maintenance of physical life in the world is not possible without our engaging in activity. So, if activity encounters us at every moment of our existence and there is no escape from its inexorable necessity, it devolves upon us to undertake it in conformity with the requirement of our spiritual nature. Only then can we hope for a happy living. We labour under a grievous delusion if we believe that happiness can come to us if we follow the path of least resistance as pointed out by our numerous desires and passions. Work must be in consonance with our inner nature, for only then can we claim to be free from all knots of bondage. Therefore, the *Gītā* says : "Not by abstention from action does a man attain freedom, nor through renunciation thereof does he attain perfection."[6] Equally deluded is he who for fear of being bound by action seeks to abstain from it. Nature is powerful enough to command obedience of its laws, and he who seeks freedom from its laws is doomed to perpetual misery and sorrow. And if, therefore, renunciation of action is not possible, abstention therefrom is sheer hypocrisy.[7] This means, then, that activity must be undertaken because it is part of the mode of human existence. Inertia or quietism is a revolt against Nature and is bound to prove abortive. Activity is the medium of the perfection of our spiritual nature and cannot be abjured under any circumstance whatever.

A particular activity becomes part of the mode of human existence when it comes to be subjected

to the determination of the law of our self, called
dharma. Thus, an action is spiritual only to the
extent to which it is determined by our dharma.
What awaited Arjuna at the battlefield of
Kurukshetra was a certain type of activity, namely,
engaging himself in a warfare. He was so much
under the influence of infatuation that he was not
prepared to accept it as his dharma. But when this
influence had completely subsided he was able to
see the futility of his desire to take to renunciation.
The law of dharma reasserted itself and Arjuna then
was able to realize that acting in accordance with
the supreme law of his self was the only way to true
peace and tranquility. If dharma has an unconditional and necessary claim on us it is cowardice,
therefore, to run away from it. Therefore, says the
Gītā, "He who does not help turn the wheel thus set
in motion in this world is evil in his nature, sensual
in his delights, and he lives in vain."[8]

When an activity is determined by the law of
our essential self it loses its natural tinge and comes
instead to be invested with a different content and
a different purpose. It is in this process of determination that it comes to be 'humanized', so to say,
and is reoriented towards a new direction. Consequently, it now derives its meaning and content
from the determination of the essential self and
becomes part of human nature (sahajamkarma).
Plato and Aristotle, the two prominent Greek
philosophers, held that man is distinguishable from
the rest of the animal world in this that, whereas the
behaviour of an animal is set for it by nature, it is
man alone who has the capacity for determining his
act by the law of his inmost being and act accord-

ingly. Thus, an action is characteristic of human nature only if it has behind it the determination of the higher self. This is what in essence the *Gītā* states here : "Far inferior indeed is mere activity to the discipline of spiritual determination, and one should, therefore, seek refuge in this discipline (buddhiyoga)."[9] The moment an activity has been subjected to the determination of the higher self, one is able to see action in inaction and inaction in action.[10]

If, according to the Gītā, neither is abandonment of work possible nor abstention from work desirable, it devolves upon us to seek our perfection through work. It is not in the renunciation *of* work, but *in* renunciation in work that true happiness can be attained. What is to be abstained from is the tendency to indulge in the gratification of our natural desires and passions, and what is to be renuonced is the tendency to hanker after the fruit of actions performed, but what is necessary is the performance of actions in the spirit of disinterestedness. This is what the divine teacher of the *Gītā* himself declares : "Therefore, without attachment perform always the actions that have to be done, for man attains to the highest by doing actions without attachment."[11] As Kant, the well-known German philosopher put it in his own way, the performance of actions without the desire for fruit is the "unconditional command which leaves the will no liberty to choose the opposite."

From what has been stated above it should not be gathered, however, that the *Gītā*, in its rigid insistence on the necessity of performing disinterested actions, enjoins the dismissal from one's mind of all motive in the doing of duty.

What must clearly be noted here is the fact that disinterested activity in the literal sense of the expression is a psychological myth and to insist upon it in the name of morality is, in Shankara's words, little short of reducing life to the form of a meaningless drudgery.[12] Will and motive cannot be torn apart. But an action to be really moral must be such that the content and authority of its motive are derived from no other source than that of the self itself. It is the self's own own law (dharma) that must find its full expression in every action : "Better indeed," says the *Gītā*, "is one's dharma than the command imposed by another. One does not incur sin when one does actions enjoined by one's own dharma."[13] In that case alone is the will not determined by anything alien to its own authority. This is what we call the moral autonomy of the individual (svadharma). This key concept pervades the entire ethical teaching of the *Gītā*. The divine teacher, Krishna, frequently enjoins upon Arjuna the necessity of following the law of his true being, of acting not in subjection to an alien law (paradharma), but in obedience to the inner determination of the soul's freedom. We have a conscious, intelligent will, and all our actions must be subjected to, and grounded in, its authority. If we fail to invest our will with such an authority and as a result act impulsively according to our likes and dislikes, the law of our true being is not worked out and thereby "we would thus be changed into mere mechanism, in which, as in a puppet-show, everything would *gesticulate* well, but there would be *no life* in the figures."[14] When, on the contrary, we succeed in disciplining our will in accordance with the demand of our inner self, there inevitably comes to supervene on us the deeper consciousness of recovered freedom. Action then becomes the source of vision of our innermost being, and the real meaning of life begins to reveal itself gradually. It is only then that disciplined activity comes to acquire the excellence of an art that must be practised in life and death.[15]

What could dispel Arjuna's doubt and destroy his delusion was a complete reorientation in his attitude toward action. So long as he could not bring his volition within the orbit of moral determination he acted only as an ignorant man and was not prepared even to listen to the voice of his higher self. All this shows how tight was the grip over his consciousness of the natural impulse which for the moment eclipsed his true self. This was only a manifestation of ajñāna or ignorance and it could be destroyed only by jñāna or true knowledge. His moral self had, it seemed, abandoned him, though only for a while. It was despondency (hridaya-daurbalyam) alone that reigned supreme over his consciousness. He was completely confused as to what he ought and what he ought not to do (dharma-sammudha-chetah). Nevertheless, the voice of duty (dharma) was ceaselessly knocking at his mind, and its source was the higher self alone. "Having regard for thine own duty (dharma) thou shouldst not falter, for there exists no greater good for a warrior than the battle enjoined by dharma. And if thou doest not this battle enjoined by dharma, thou shalt fail in thy dharma and incur sin."[16] It was only by embracing the true law of dharma that he was able to regain his self and declared : "Destroyed is my delusion and recognition has been gained by me through thy grace, O Krishna. I now stand firm with my doubts dispelled. I shall act according to thy word."[17] He was now completely possessed of his true self, having successfully effected a break from his natural, emotional self. He thereby was able to rise to a truly universal ethical perspective whereby he alone could fulfil the demand of his dharma. He was now in a position to do what his dharma objectively required him to do.

4. *My station and its duties*

The only justification for the rise of the *Gītā* was its desire to expound the philosophy of a new social order based on the specialization of functions. Arjuna, the hero of the *Gītā*, is a member of the warrior class and he has certain duties relative to his station in life. Each individual, we are told, is born with a particular station in his society. Of necessity certain duties devolve upon us the performance of which is inextricably and necessarily liked up with the attainment of perfection.[18] Naturally, perfection becomes the prerogative of one who has disciplined and enlightened his will by selflessly discharging the duties that pertain to his station, whoever he is and whatever is his station. It is not *what* we do, but *how* we do what we do that really matters. God, as someone has aptly said, "cares more for the adverb than for the verb." A soldier, for instance, has, in conformity with the nature of the work he is obliged to do, a determinate code of conduct set for him (svadharma). It is quite conceivable that at times the discharging of his duties may entail much hardship and suffering, as in the case of Arjuna at the battlefield of Kurukshetra. But is he justified in abstaining from discharging his duties on such grounds ? Decidedly not, says the *Gītā*. For, it requires us to continue our work, in both perfect and imperfect conditions of life. Abandonment of work is not contemplated in the *Gītā* at any stage of life. Absence of conscientious devotion to work, whatever it is that has fallen to our lot, is looked upon in the Gītā as reprehensible.[19] The soldier who has wilfully ignored the law of his being (svadharma) has forfeited the claim of his will to what is true autonomy and freedom, thereby allowing it to be subjected to the alien authority of natural impulses and emotions (paradharma). True renunciation is possible when we are detached in our attitude and perform our duties as the demand of our ethical self. The *Gītā* cites three kinds of renunciation that an active man may resort to. Firstly, he may renounce an obligatory act through delusion, but this is positively dangerous, for it will obstruct the manifestation of his inner self. Secondly, he may come to renounce a duty because it entails with it much suffering, mental or physical or even both; but renunciation of this kind can never bring true happiness and freedom. And, lastly only that individual is entitled to everlasting peace and tranquility who performs his duty solely because it ought to be done, irrespective of all extraneous considerations. Possessed of the autonomy of his soul, he never abhors a duty because of the disagreeable consequences the performance thereof may be attended with.[20] Such a renunciation is true sacrifice and

such an agent is a man of true renunciation
(samnyāsin). In thus working in response to the
voice of his self he finds his true happiness. Work
is undertaken by him for the service of others, but
without any hope for recompense. Service of
humanity through the performance of duty, according to the *Gītā*, is the real service to God, and from
the ultimate point of view, a service to one's own
cause.[21]

5. *The three froms of dharma*

Goodness, according to the *Gītā*, may express
itself in three different, well defined grades or levels,
the difference in each case being ascertainable in
terms of the position the self occupies in relation to
the actual process of volition. First, the manifestation of goodness is certainly at its lowest ebb when
the act of volition comes to be determined by some
remote desire for pleasure, such as in the observance
of the Vedic rituals with a view to attaining heaven
(svarga-prāpti). Although such actions do not
deserve to be characterized as good in the real
sense of the term inasmuch as they do not involve,
and are not the result of, conscious determination,
yet they do entail some amount of sacrifice of the
immediate prompting of the sensuous self and thereby serve as the occasion for stirring up that
conscious conflict wherein lies the future possibility
of choice of goodness. That, it seems, is the only
ground on which almost all the Hindu texts and
schools can, and do, base their justification for
permitting the performance of the Vedic rituals.
Hence, God, in the *Gītā*, comes to be accepted as of
necessity a complemenentary agency to bring about

the fruition of such performances. Secondly, an action that has been performed in conscious determination is relatively good, but it is through such an action that the process of sacrifice is to be consummated in the realization of the pure identity of the self. And, lastly, an action is unconditionally good when it is the outcome of an absolutely self-determined being, and it is in this sense that the *Gītā* speaks of a man of true realization (sthita-prajña). It is also in this sense that God comes to be described as the embellishment and essence of dharma.

The important point to note in the present context is that, while explaining the ideal of spiritual enlightenment (moksha) the *Gītā* falls completely in line with the Upanishads. It is in its attempt to work out the details of the concept of dharma that it purports to break a new ground. In its view, dharma is not only the motive of all ethical activity but also the ideal thereof. Thus looked at, dharma becomes the highest state worthy of realization by all those actions that involve it as their motive-force. Since the self is regarded as the very essence and embodiment of dharma, naturally the goal comes to be described in terms of the realization by the self as itself the very form of dharma. It is here, then, that the *Gītā* emphatically declares: "Swiftly does the self become of the form of dharmātman, and it then attains everlasting bliss."[22] This is declared to be the supreme state of realization which dawns when dharma has reached the highest stage of its fruition.[23] And, insofar as God, like the self, is the very representation of dharma, the goal to be attained may also be described as the soul's attaining equivalence with the dharma of the Divine

Will.[24]   A will that has come to rise as high as the objective spirit of dharma will necessarily act from sheer love for goodness.   Its maxim of action will necessarily be universal in appeal and application. The principle of its action will be one on which I and you—in fact, all human beings—would act without fear of contradiction.   Duty, as ordinarily understood, would shed its obligatoriness (na tasya kāryam vidyate), and the liberated man would act in a spirit of sheer spontaneity and ease.   As Shankara said, "In the case of a person who has awakened to a knowledge of the self, virtues like kindness involve no conscious effort.   They become part and parcel of his nature."[25]   In other words, there is complete correspondence between the spirit of dharma and that of the liberated soul, so that what is objectively right is done as right.

6. *God as an ideal karma-yogin*

The interesting point about the *Gītā* is that it believes every living being to be in one way or other responsive to activity that sweeps the entire world.   Even God cannot be regarded as enjoying complete impunity from activity.   But there is a difference between man and God inasmuch as the former acts in a way in which the latter does not by virtue of his purely spiritual nature.   Unlike God, man's will is erratic and arbitrary, and he may, therefore, act or not act according to dharma.   God, on the contrary, ever acts in the spirit of dharma by virtue of his nature as purely spiritual.   God is thus ever active and is in this sense an ideal karma-yogin. While man has to attain to such an ideal state through his efforts, God is already in that state.

This is the ideal which the *Gītā* asks us to attain in order to be worthy of true happiness.

In the eyes of the *Gītā*, God as the embodiment of dharma is the ideal karma-yogin. He acts in and through the world which is his body. He is ever active in the creation and maintenance of the world, having nothing to realize for himself. "There is," says the *Gītā*'s God, "nothing in the three worlds which has to be done, nor anything to be obtained, yet I am ever engaged in activity."[26] All activity (karma), as we know, originates in the world of matter, and God on his part brings to bear upon it the law of absolute rational determination. It is by means of this law that he determines the course of events in the physical universe, and that is precisely why it exhibits complete harmony and law-abidingness. It is not erratic and arbitrary like the human activity, since behind it is the sanction of the law of spiritual determination. As pure Spirit, God remains unaffected by the world. "No activity," says the Divine Being of the *Gītā*, "defiles me, nor do I have any yearning for its fruit. He who knows me thus is not bound by activity."[27] Bondage is another name for allowing oneself to be passively determined by the desire for fruit of actions, but when performed without attachment to its fruit, every action becomes a sacrifice. "Except for action performed as a sacrifice, this world is in bondage. Therefore, O Arjuna, do thy action as a sacrifice, becoming free from all attachments."[28] It is in this sense that the *Gītā* speaks of sacrifice (yajña) as having been born of activity (karma).[29] When we have given up all attachments and our will becomes the medium of unobstructed manifestation of our inmost being, we cease to arrogate to ourselves the agency of all the deeds and are then in a position to see that it is the physical universe alone (prakriti) that is active. Although we seem to be doing one thing or other, we are really not doing anything. The soul is a mere witness, and what is active is just the world around us. This is what is to be realized for ourselves, for so long as we look upon ourselves as active we cannot help arrogating to ourselves the agency of all that is done. Yet we should ever employ ourselves in work, not because we like to have the fruit thereof but because without it we cannot live in the world and attain our true purpose. God is ever active and his aim is to keep the world going in accordance with its own causes and conditions. And if God did not act what would be the result ? The result, says the *Gītā*, "would be that these worlds would fall in ruin, and I shall be called the cause of all confusion and chaos."[30]

It means, then, that God as an ideal karma-yogin is deeply involved in all the activities and functions of the world. "All that is here," says Krishna, "is strung on me as rows of gems on a string."[31] God is transcendent to the world insofar as activity is foreign to his nature, but is immanent in it because nothing can be active unless activity itself is yoked to the determination of his ever perfect spirit. "By me all this universe is pervaded through my unmanifest form. All beings abide in me, but I do not abide in them."[23] Since activity necessarily presupposes spiritual determination and *vice versa*, God and the world cannot be conceived as in any sense separable. God as the principle of spiritual determination must be ever active so as to invest his will with a content, while the world, in order to be ever creative, must be subject to spiritual determination. The world needs God as much as God needs the world. "This is my lower nature," says Krishna, "know my other and higher nature which is the Spirit by which this world is upheld."[33]

To conclude : man is as much possessed of dharma as God is, but both differ in respect of the degrees with which each exhibits it in activity. God as the perfection of the spirit of dharma ever acts for the good of the world and maintains it both in its moral and physical aspects. Dharma is the law of spiritual determination, while karma is the ground for such a determination. The world manifests both in different spheres. Neither God nor the world can subsist by itself, since activity without spiritual determination is blind, while spiritual determination without activity is empty. Buddhism retains only activity and rejects the agent. This is one extreme. Those who preach the path of renunciation and reject activity represent another extreme. To quote Radhakrishnan, "The man of the world is lost in the varied activities of the world. He throws himself into the mutable world (kshara). The quietist withdraws into the silence of the Absolute (akshara), but the ideal man of the *Gītā* goes beyond these two extremes and works like Purushottama who reconciles all possibilities in the world without getting involved in it. He is the doer of works who yet is not the doer, kartāramakartāram. The Lord is the pattern of an unwearied and active worker who does not by his work forfeit his integrity of spirit."[34]

Thesis, antithesis, and synthesis

When we cast our glance at the entire development of the early Hindu ethical thought we come across three main currents : the thesis of the Veda, antithesis of the Upanishads, and the synthesis of the *Gītā*. And it is in this that lies the uniqueness of the *Gītā*. Not many scholars have emphasized this point. Let us, therefore, briefly touch upon this point.

1. The Vedic Thesis. The Veda teaches the performance of rituals as a means to the attainment of certain worldly goods. This is called karma-kānḍa. The main thing is that certain actions are enjoined to be performed for the sake of certain results.

2. The Upanishadic Antithesis. As we have pointed out before, the Upanishads emphasize renunciation as a means to bringing about the end of bondage of karma. It was believed that, since all karma was a potent source of bondage, salvation could be possible by renouncing it. The last two stages of life (āshramas) were devised with this end in view—those of vānaprastha and saṁnyāsa. Thus, whereas the Veda accepted the positive path of worldly participation, the Upanishads, on the other hand, emphasized the negative path of renunciation. And the two are *prima facie* exclusive of each other.

3. The *Gītā* Synthesis. The *Gītā* provides a fine specimen of the synthesis of both these paths. It accepts the Vedic view that karma is to be performed, but rejects the other part thereof, namely, that it should be undertaken for the sake of its results.

On the other hand, the *Gītā* retains the Upanishadic view that renunciation must be a necessary constituent of every man's active life. But it teaches that this could best be practised when one performs one's action without the desire for the fruit thereof. It is, then, not renunciation of karma, but renunciation in karma that brings out the true ethical ideal worthy of realization by every man. What is, therefore, to be renounced is not karma but its fruit. What causes bondage is not mere action but the desire for its fruit. A life of activity is fully compatible with man's desire for salvation. Quietism or inertia is, therefore, condemned by the *Gītā* in no unequivocal terms. Thus looked at, karma-yoga provides a synthesis, with its own meaning and implication. And it is this that consists the uniqueness of the *Gītā* as an ethical treatise.

References

1. For a fuller exposition see my *Essence of Bhagavad-Gītā* (Arnold-Heinemann : 1981).
2. I. ii. 11.
3. BG., iv. 17.
4. iv. 16.
5. iii. 5 ; xviii. 11, 59.
6. iii. 4.
7. iii. 6.
8. iii. 16.
9. ii. 49.
10. iv. 18.
11. iii. 19.
12. Commentary on BG., iii. 1.
13. BG., iii. 35.
14. *Kant's Critique of Practical Reason* (Abbott's translation), p. 245.

15. BG., ii. 50.
16. ii. 31-33.
17. xi. 51, xviii. 73.
18. xviii. 45.
19. xviii. 47.
20. xviii. 7-10.
21. xviii. 46.
22. ix. 31.
23. ix. 2.
24. xiv. 2. Mama sādharmyam āgataḥ.
25. *Naishkarmya-sidhhi*, iv. 69.
26. BG., iii. 9.
27. iv. 14.
28. iii. 9.
29. iv. 32.
30. iii. 24.
31. vii. 7.
32. ix-4-5.
33. vii. 5.
34. S. Radhakrishnan, *The Bhagavad-gītā* (London : George Allen & Unwin, 1948). p. 72.

Chapter VIII

THE UPANISHADS AND LATER
INDIAN THOUGHT

The four Vedas—Rig, Yajur, Sāma and
Atharva—constitute the basic structure of the entire
Indian thought. All subsequent developments are
often traced to them. The Upanishads arose with a
view to emphasizing and elaborating their metaphysical point of view loosely knit and casually presented
at different places of their sections. The profundity
of insights and lucidity of exposition so conspicuously encountered in their exposition have no parallel in the entire history of the development of the
Indian tradition in philosophy. One simply
marvels at the philosophic ingenuity of the Indians
many thousands of years before. The *Bhagavad-Gītā*
represents the process of continuity of the Vedic
tradition and arose to supplement the earlier
thought on the ethical front. The way it sought to
provide a unique synthesis of the various loose
elements of the preceding period entitles
it to be ranked as perhaps the best treatise on
Hindu view and way of life. The aim was to build
up an ethics of action through a process of combination of those elements that had practically
received little attention at the hands of the earlier
seers of the Vedic age. Thus looked at, both the
Upanishads and the *Gītā* arose not to reject anything
of the old but to rebuild a new edifice on the found-
ations of the old. This shows that the Vedic Indian

was ever alive to the changing needs of the society and sought to orient his teaching in accordance with them. He seemed to be well aware of the fact that human conduct was as much subject to the process of evolution and growth as the physical universe itself and needed constant vigilance to keep it on the right track. The Vedas, the Upanishads and the *Gītā* thus constitute one single tradition and contributed substantially to the growth of the subsequent Indian thought. While the Upanishads profoundly influenced it on the metaphysical front, the *Gītā* made its impact felt on almost every system or school that arose in course of time.

The bewildering diversity of the schools that arose subsequent to the Vedic tradition has been divided into two parts: the orthodox (āstika), and the heterodox (nāstika). The former are those that owe allegiance to the Vedic tradition and accept it as the model of their reasoning. The latter, on the contrary, are those that embark upon an independent course, seeking to justify their conclusions by means of their own reasoning. Those schools that claim to accept the Vedic authority are Nyāya, Vaisheshika, Sānkhya, Yoga, the Mīmānsā and the various branches of the Vedānta, notably Shankara's Advaita-Vedānta, and Rāmānuja's Vishishṭādvaita. Jainism, Chārvāka and Buddhism are representatives of the heterodox tradition.

Our aim in this chapter is to show how and to what extent, if any, the Upanishadic metaphysics influenced the later Indian thought. Only then could it be possible to show the metaphysics of the Upanishads in its true perspective. We first take up the three schools of the heterodox tradition.

The heterodox tradition

The one important question which almost all the Indian systems of philosophy accorded top priority is: What is that method of enquiry which, when employed in philosophical investigations, can give us indubitable results? In other words, that knowledge alone could be accepted as infallible which was acquired through a rational method of enquiry. The Upanishads argued that the only method available for philosophical investigations was thought, but what at best it could lead us to was the concept of Being (sat), and its opposite, viz., that of Non-being (asat). As we know, while the multiplicity of things was revealed by the various senses it was through thought alone that Being could be apprehended. We could easily think all beings away, but Being itself could not be thought away. So both Being and Non-being are the ultimate categories of thought in terms of which the entire universe of our experience and activity could be explained. But such a universe must be relative, determined in its behaviour by the laws. The Upanishads here assert that, while such a universe cannot be the ultimate truth of our experience because it is subject to the determination of its laws, knowledge must not stop short of an absolute and unconditioned stage. This, as we have seen, is what the Upanishads understand by 'transcendent knowledge' (parā-vidyā). Being and Non-being belong to the conceptual order and cannot, therefore, yield knowledge of the absolute and the unconditioned. The Jainas fully agree with this approach and argue in their own way that the highest object of all philosophic quest must be the absolute knowledge (kevala-jñāna). And such a knowledge can be acquired by transcending all the limitations of ordinary knowledge. Accordingly, the Jainas undertake an analysis or critique of ordinary knowledge and seek to show that it does not reveal more than what forms its content. The moment we seek to stretch it beyond the realm of experience we arrive at the notion of the indescribable. In this context we shall mention here the Jaina theory of knowledge, called saptabhangī-naya. There are in it seven steps, and the conclusion is that whatever way we proceed we end up in a state which is simply indescribable. This theory may be stated in its bare outlines thus :

A is (asti).

A is not (nāsti).

A is and is not (asti nāsti cha).

A is indescribable (avaktavyam).

A is and is indescribable (asti cha avaktav-yam).

A is not and is indescribable (nāsti cha avak-tavyam).

A is, is not, and is indescribable (asti, nāsti cha avaktavyam).

What the Jainas seek to show is that Being and Non-being are simply conceptual representations and cannot apply to a description of the transcendent reality. So, the ultimate reality is simply indescri-bable. So long as we continue to rely on thought as a tool of philosophical investigations the ultimate truth must remain simply indescribable. And when through our efforts we are able to transcend all the limitations of ordinary knowledge we have an infi-nite knowledge whereby nothing is left out of our

apprehension. This is the stage of omniscience. The
omniscient being knows all that there is as reality.
There is nothing like an absolute Spirit of the Upanishadic conception nor any personal agency like
God over and above an omniscient soul. And when
the infinite knowledge dawns there is infinite bliss,
infinite power, infinite faith, and infinite vision. The
soul begins to shine in its natural integrity and
knows itself as what it is in its pristine glory and
perfection. It then transcends all limitations of the
spatio-temporal world (lokākāsha) and ever abides
in its own autonomy and identity. There is no
rebirth, since the soul comes to be dissociated from
all selfish propensities, desires and passions. In itself it attains to the state of immortality. It is truly
its own, having disowned all that is not its own. It
retains its individuality, but maintains it for all time
to come. The Jainas regard all the liberated souls
as objects of worship. They leave behind them
noble ideals to inspire those trailing behind on the
path of spiritual pilgrimage.

The other heterodox school to be briefly considered here is Chārvāka. It preaches materialism.
Its fundamental point of view is that matter alone is
the ultimate truth and that everything else encountered in our experience and activity can be explained in terms of matter and its laws. There is no self
as understood by the Upanishads and the Jainas.
Consciousness is an offshoot of matter. It arises at
the time of birth and extinguishes itself at the time
of death. There is, therefore, nothing like the state
of liberation. The universe is at heart a mechanical
and blind interplay of physical forces and it has been
going on in its course from all eternity. There is

no ethics in the sense as understood in the conventional sense. Pleasure alone is the only *summum bonum* of life. It is the ethics which teaches 'Eat, drink and be merry'. Life is short and one can make the best out of it by enjoying the various things that afford it satisfaction. This is virtually another extreme. If the Upanishads accept the self alone as the ultimate truth, the Chārvāka materialists take matter to be the ultimate reality about man and the universe and seek to explain everything in terms thereof. But the Chārvāka-materialism could not muster enough support from any quarter and remains a most ignominious form of a crude philosophy. The tide of the Upanishadic philosophy was adequate enough to sweep it off its current without any difficulty. So, not much is known about this materialistic thought.

Buddhism is the other heterodox school which as a whole made a very deep impact on the development of the subsequent course of Indian philosophy. Buddha was the founder of this school which branched off in many directions of thought. When Buddha was asked many different questions of metaphysics, such as those relating to the ultimate truth, the nature of soul, the state of spiritual prefection, etc., he kept silent, indicating thereby that all such questions could not be answered in the way in which they were asked. So, all transcendentalism of the Upanishadic sort was not relevant to him. Instead, he advised all his disciples not to waste their time in discussing notions of Being and Non-being. Experience — concrete, living experience — for him was the starting point. And what did such an experience teach? he asked. It revealed a world characterized by becoming, change, movement. It was a

world ever in the process of onward motion or creation. So, a thing did not stay the same even for two
moments. This view is called "momentariness"
(kshaṇika-vāda). All is, therefore, destined to change.
We are born, we live, and then die. It is through
ignorance that we get attached to different things
and fondly believe that they are permanent in af-
fording us satisfaction. Even if they are imperma-
nent, we wish them to be otherwise. It is clinging
and nothing more. We cling to things, not knowing
that they are subject to destruction. Attachments
and aversions overtake us and cause our bondage.
We fall into the process of transmigration, being
born and dying in an endless chain. This can stop
only when we cleanse ourselves of all our defile-
ments. We can break the chain of physical causation only by resorting to what is generally known as
the "Eight-fold Path". It consists of right views,
right resolve, right speech, right conduct, right live-
lihood, right mindfulness, right conduct and right
concentration. This is the middle way "which enlightens the eyes, enlightens the mind, which leads
to rest, to knowledge, to enlightenment, to Nirvāṇa."

The difference between the Upanishads on the
one hand, and Buddha on the other is one of approach. Whereas, as we know, the former begin
with the nature of self, the latter begins with the
not-self and seeks to accomplish the same result as
the former do. According to an Upanishad, no
longer extant, the self is nothing but silence (upashānto'yam ātmā). Buddha translated this teaching
into practice and maintained tight-lipped silence
when certain ultimate questions were put to him.
According to him, what lies beyond all speech and

is indescribable in any human language cannot be a
matter of discussion or dispute. The ultimate truth
can at best be a matter of practical realization. For
Buddha it is nirvāṇa, or in the language of the
Vedānta, moksha.

Soon after Buddha's death the movement faced a
split. Two different schools arose—one that sought to
adhere faithfully to Buddha's original teaching, called
Hīnayāna, and the other that engaged itself in the
analysis of the various implications of Buddha's teaching, known as Mahāyāna. The Mahāyānists held
that their master's silence was not the *denial* of any
transcendent reality, but was meant to indicate the
incomprehensibility thereof through any ordinary
human mode. The Mahāyāna school split into two
parts and gave rise to two closely allied sub-schools,
known as Vijñāna-vāda or Yogāchāra, and the
Mādhyamika or Shūnya-vāda. According to the
former, vijñāna or pure consciousness is the ultimate
truth, a view in no way different from that of the
Upanishads. The world is declared to be a false
appearance (māyā), a mere superimposition on the
cosmic consciousness. The outer world is a mere
projection of the thought-forms much the same way
as the dream-ideas are projected outside so as to
create a world. In this sense the world is a mere
creation of our ideas. The truth dawns only when
the spiritual aspirant is able to see pure consciousness not through any thought-form but directly and
immediately as one's own essence and truth.

The other school, Shūnya-vāda, seeks to be
more critical in reaching the same result. It developed a very vigorous method of enquiry, a dialectic
whereby the exponents of this school sought to show

that all the categories of thought are vitiated by self-contradiction. All such categories — such as self, causation, relation — apply only to the phenomenal world and it can be interpreted in terms thereof. But when we apply these categories in explaining the ultimate facts of knowledge these categories bring us the results which are self-contradictory. The dialectical method comprises four steps (chatush-koṭi): Being, Non-being, neither both nor ñeither. First a certain thesis is taken up for consideration. And when it does not go far, its opposite is considered. And when the antithesis, too, is found to be not of much help, both the thesis and the antithesis are sought to be combined. In any case, the result is the same. All categories are found to be attended with results that are ultimately contradictory and, therefore, not fit for application in the pursuit of the transcendent.

The state of perfection is not definable either as the creation of something new or the discarding of something old. It cannot be regarded as some positive state of being, for all positive states, being the outcome of cooperative causes, are liable to the processes of decay and destruction. Nor can it be characterized as a negative state, for if it is not a positive one, it cannot be negative either. The fact is that its true meaning can be apprehended only when all the relative standpoints have been transcended. It is at best describable as that which transcends all forms of human characterization or standpoint. It does not admit of any human predications of being and non-being. The real is indeterminable (shūnya) because all determinations are thought-constructs. From a certain point of view such an interpretation may be said to be basically

Upanishadic in character. As we have already seen, the Upanishads take sufficient pains to show that Brahman or the absolute Spirit is beyond all conceptual categories of Being and Non-being. Guided by the results of its dialectical method, the Shūnya-vādins cannot state that the Absolute is or is not, for then it becomes part of the conceptual order. In order to see what the real is we must feel it, as it were, in a non-dual form of knowledge (advayam-jñānam). This is the reality which can be brought about only when there is the total change in our perspective towards its true nature. Here the real and the realization thereof coincide so intimately that there remains not even the remotest possibility of any differences of the two. In this state prajñā is the ultimate truth. Even the world, when looked at from this standpoint, is the Absolute. When viewed through the forms of conceptual determination the Absolute will appear as the phenomenal world (sansāra), and when it is looked at through spiritual realization it is Nirvāṇa. We are said to know the truth when we are able to know ourselves as the Absolute. Nothing new is brought into existence nor anything old is shed away. It is being what one ever has been.

The one noteworthy feature of this school is its tendency to explain the phenomenal by seeking to reduce the Absolute to the level of thought (samvriti-satya). In this respect it is called dharma. This is but another way of saying that dharma is the Absolute of our conceptual determination. Buddha is spoken of as having descended on earth to preach compassion (karuṇā) for all sentient beings. Consequently, he comes to be conceived as the unity of three embodiments (kāyas), each having its specific principle of explanation. Thus, Buddha is dharma-kāya, or the embodiment of dharma in precisely the same sense in which God in Hinduism is the embodiment of dharma; he is sambhoga-kāya, or the embodiment of all blissful experience, as in the state of perfection; and he is nirmāṇa-kāya, or the creative force behind the world. Buddha as the embodiment of dharma is its very perfection or its very realization (dharma-prāpta). He is in this sense a personal God to whom innumerable powers and merits are ascribed. Whatever is willed by him is in strict conformity with the objective spirit of dharma. As such, he is the reality of all that claims to be (dharma-dhātu). As sambhoga-kāya he is conceived as the embellishment of all those auspicious qualities which the human heart cherishes in its dissatisfaction with the world around him. Here is the Supreme Being dwelling in heaven, enjoying the sweet company of a host of buddhas (liberated souls). The various perfections attributed to the Buddha-God are regarded as the highest that man can attain to in his pursuit of the good. As nirmāṇa-kāya, Buddha is looked upon as endowed with volition which expresses itself as a creative agency behind the dynamic character of the universe. It is by virtue of this creative volition that Buddha assumes cosmic forms and appears in the world as its saviour. Concern for the emancipation of all beings is conceived as one of the most prominent traits of Buddha's personality. In sheer compassion for all living beings he incarnates himself so as to pull them out of the mire of suffering. It is because of this intense desire to liberate all these beings (sarva-mukti) that makes him "mahākaruṇā", or the most compassionate. Gautama is one of an endless series of Buddhas to descend on earth for the emancipation of all sentient beings. "No activity of the Buddhas is without reason. Their very birth is for the good of all creatures." "Therefore, all Buddhas, in order to emancipate sentient beings from misery, are inspired with great spiritual energy and mingle themselves in the filth of birth and death. Though thus they make themselves subject to the laws of birth and death, their hearts are free from sin and attachments. They are like unto those immaculate, undefiled lotus flowers which grow out of mire, yet are not contaminated by it."[1]

It is now abundantly clear that Mahāyāna Buddhism bears a striking similarity to the Upanishadic thought. Both in respect of the method of enquiry and the results, the two systems might seem to run parallel to each other. While the Upanishads were concerned more with the statement of results, the Māhayāna-Buddhists sought to develop and devise a method that could lead them to certain indubitable results. Happily enough, these results turn out to be almost the same as those reached by the Upanishads. The dialectical method gave Buddhism a sound base and put the results on a very rational footing. There is, then, little doubt that the two traditions have philosophized to such depths that were not fathomed by the subsquent thinkers of India. Absolute idealism, therefore, remained the key-note of Indian tradition in philosophy.

The orthodox tradition

There arose, in course of time, certain systems of Indian philosophy which were not as thorough-going in methodology and results as their predecessors. Though they claim to owe allegiance to the Vedic tradition, yet this allegiance is only nominal. They do not generally share much of the philosophizing of the Upanishads. The Vaisheshika, Sānkhya, and the Mimānsā are atheists. The Nyāya and Yoga are certainly theists, but their theism does not mean much. God is a mere hypothesis. He is invented to fit into certain situations that are otherwise inexplicable. So, we need not consider these schools here.

However, the Upanishadic tradition found in Shankara a strong supporter, a mature logician, a dialectician, and above all, an exponent of its spirit. His contention is that Brahman is simply indescribable (anirvachanīya) in terms of any human concept or category. The two categories of Being and Non-being cannot be applied to what is of the nature of pure consciousness. Brahman alone is the absolute truth; the soul is in essence the very nature of Brahman, and the world is a mere false appearance (māyā). Let us explain this view by reference to the stock example of the rope and the snake. A man mistakes a rope for a snake under cover of darkness. He cries out for help and someone rushes to his rescue. But what is subsequently found there is not the snake but only a rope. But how did the rope appear to the victim to be a snake ? Did the rope actually get transformed into the shape of the snake ? Certainly not. The rope has ever remained so throughout his experience. It means, then, that the discrepancy in perceiving the rope as something else arose in the mind of the experient. There lay dormant in his subconsciousness the old impres-

sion of the nature of the snake which was easily
revived because of the close similarity between the
rope and the snake. What actually happened was
that the snake-form was inadvertently superimposed
(adhyāsa) on the rope as existing in its own objectivity. Thus, instead of viewing the rope as rope he
misperceived it as a snake. What does all this
mean ? asks Shankara. Firstly, it means that all
illusions are cases of superimpositions. An old idea
in the mind comes to be superimposed on an object
that really exists out of mind. Secondly, in all such
cases there is the unmistakable manifestation of the
ignorance about the true nature of the underlying
reality. And, lastly, ignorance (avidyā, ajñāna) not
only conceals the real nature of the underlying object but also makes it appear as something else
instead.

When thus understood, Brahman is the ultimate truth but under human limitations we take it
to be something else, namely, the world. What
we call the world is, then, nothing more than a
creation of our thought. We superimpose upon
Brahman something of our ignorant mind as a result
of which it comes to appear as something else. So
long as we are what we are, such impositions constitute our outlook and attitude and we cannot but
take the world to be real. Just as in a case of opti-
cal illusion there is an underlying object which
reveals its true nature when we have the correct
perspective, so underlying all our experiences and
activities there is the one, all-pervasive Spirit which
can reveal its nature when we approach it with a
correct and adequate point of view.

Shankara holds that we have three different experiences from three different points of view: the standpoint of the mere appearance (prātibhāsika); that of actual experience as in the waking condition (vyāvahārika); and, lastly, that of transcendence (pāramārthika). From the standpoint of mere appearance, an object is mistaken for another at the mere sensory level, as the rope is mistaken for a snake. From the standpoint of practical experience, the world is taken to be real for all practical purposes. But here, too, ignorance of the underlying object characterizes all our outlook and attitude. It is in our belief of the reality of the world that we develop attachments (rāga) and aversions (dvesha) and bring about our bondage by acting in determination thereof. This bondage can be brought to an end only when we ascend to the highest standpoint where we are just of the very nature of Brahman. In order to limelight this point Shankara distinguishes between the two conceptions of Brahman: the one from which Brahman is known as Brahman and all distinctions disappear for good. This is the objective approach from which Brahman is known in his intrinsic qualities (svarūpa-lakshaṇa). But when we seek to view it from our ordinary point of view he is taken to be as the creator, sustainer, and the destroyer of the universe. Brahman, when thus conceived, is the personal God whom we worship and of whom favours are asked. This is the unnatural conception of Brahman (taṭastha-lakshaṇa). Shankara seeks to illustrate this point in this way. A shepherd is assigned the role of a king in a certain drama. He wears the robe of a king and appears on the stage as a king. He wages war against other countries, conquers them, and establishes his rule. Now, the description of the actor as a shepherd refers to what he is from the intrinsic point of view. Such a description is from the point of view of his true characteristic (svarūpalakshaṇa). But the description of him as a king is only valid from the standpoint of mere appearance (taṭastha-lakshaṇa). From this point of view, then, both God and the world are not the true descriptions of the ultimate truth. Brahman does not admit of any human representation and in whatever way he is humanly described is utterly inadequate to his intrinsic nature.

The human soul, according to Shankara as according to the Upanishads, is of the very essence of Brahman. Therefore, liberation consists in the soul's realization of itself as the very truth of Brahman. Shankara reminds us that Brahman is of the nature of real (sat), pure consciousness (chit), and unique bliss (ānanda). When the soul is able to effect complete union with Brahman it finds itself possessed of supreme bliss. All its past karmas having been burnt in the fire of spiritual knowledge, it abides in infinite bliss. According to Shankara, a person who has attained enlightenment will continue to be associated with his body only so long as his past deeds so require. And this means that liberation (moksha) is attainable within the span of a particular human life. So long as the enlightened man remains associated with his body he will work for the reconstruction of his society as taught in the *Gītā*. He will act, but from sheer ease of his spirit, for he is completely free from the constraint of duty. He will say 'I will', not 'I ought'. This stage of liberation is called

'Jivan-mukti'. But when the liberated soul discards
the physical frame of the body it finds itself as what
it has realized already. This stage of liberation is
called 'videha-mukti'. The soul thereupon attains
immortality and has no birth or death. It retraces
its step to what it has ever been. It is being Brahman. It has now transcended all, becoming characteristics of the world of all ignorant beings. It is
now truly a soul in the state of its intrinsic reality,
pure consciousness and blissful experience
(sachchidānanda).[2]

Rāmānuja followed close on the heels of Shankara in the interpretation of the Vedānta philosophy
of the Upanishads. But he disagreed with him on
many important points. Rāmānuja rejects outright
Shankara's notion of Brahman as pure being, devoid
of all qualifications (nirguṇa-brahma). His contention was that such a being is a mere fiction. In his
view, to speak of Brahman as pure consciousness,
existence, and bliss (sachchidānanda) amounts to
attributing to Brahman certain qualities, and this
clearly means that even Shankara could not help
conceiving of Brahman as in some way qualified
(saguṇa). If, says Rāmānuja, Brahman is to be conceived as existent he must exist with certain qualities, and this should mean, therefore, that Brahman
exists as a concrete, positive Being. Hence, in his
view, Brahman can only be conceived as qualified,
and not as absolutely devoid of all qualifications.

God (Brahman), according to Rāmānuja, is,
then, a concrete whole of which the unconscious
matter (achit) and the conscious souls (chit) are the
inalienable parts. The former is the cause of all the

material things encountered here and now by the conscious souls. It is called prakriti. It is real in its own right and essence, and is controlled by God very much the same way as the human body is controlled from within by the human soul. The latter are equally real in their own right and essence. They are also controlled by God who dwells in them as their ultimate Master (antaryāmin). They are parts of God insofor as they are essentially conscious, but insofar as they are finite they are unlike him. However, they are free to act and their destiny is, therefore, guided by their past deeds. They are in bondage because of their conditioned deeds.

Since God is the controller of the physical universe, it has come into existence because of his power of creation. Rāmānuja quotes the *Shvetāshvatara Upanishad* as holding that God is the wielder of māyā because it is through this inherent power of his that he creates and controls the world of material things. Therefore, māyā, for Rāmānuja, means not a mere source of cosmic illusion, as it is taken to mean by Shankara, but God's power of creating wonderful objects. The whole of the realm of material objects is in this sense a māyā. Thus looked at, there is nothing like a cosmic illusion but a world of physical things real in their own essence. God is the ultimate reality in the universe in the sense that there is no other reality outside or independent of him. Both the material objects and the finite souls coexist in his nature as the controller. The one is the unique synthesis of the many, all existent in a certain relation. Therefore, this monism of Rāmānuja is known as Vishishṭādvaita. It is suggestive of the Unity of parts, all in some way qualified by certain specific qualities and bound in certain specific relationships.

According to Rāmānuja, God is possessed of an infinite number of infinitely good or auspicious qualities, such as compassion (dayā). He is omnipotent, omniscient, benevolent. He responds to all our prayers and expects all his devotees to reach him through the different paths of knowledge, action, and faith. All the three disciplines have their own presuppositions and are, therefore, not to be practised by all alike. And this is taken to mean that only the members of the three upper classes of Hindu society —viz., Brāhmins, Kshatriyas, and Vaishyas—qualify themselves for practising them. Obviously, such a course not only narrows down the universal appeal of all the disciplines but also allows only a select few the privilege to make them the pathway to God. Keeping this limitation in view, Rāmānuja worked out a comparatively simpler scheme of spiritual living which could be adopted by any one, irrespective of caste, creed, or profession. This scheme is called "prapatti" (absolute surrender to God) or "Sharaṇāgati" (seeking refuge in God). The discipline of prapatti enjoins upon the devotee 'to follow the will of God, to renounce all that incurs his displeasure, generate full faith in him as the saviour of all, seek help from him alone, and sacrifice all that one possesses for him in a spirit of meekness'. The text sums up the characteristics of a prapanna thus: 'A prapanna is one who has sought refuge in God, and God alone, feels utterly helpless, and is without any other refuge'. The basis of prapatti is the unswerving conviction that God has boundless compassion for the erring man and is ever actuated by the desire to show mercy to him (nirhetuka-kripā), if the latter has sincerely resolved to seek refuge unto him. Of special mention here, however, is Rāmā-nuja's conception of what he calls 'ārta-prapatti', a feeling of absolute self-surrender in times of distress. It is in moments of extreme agony and anguish that the devotee finds himself most near to God. A single psychological moment of such a feeling of nearness may be quite sufficient to bring about his deliverance from the knots of bondage. It is in such a moment that the devotee ecstatically exclaims: "I am thy holy divinity and thou art myself'. This is the simplest and also easiest pathway to the holy divine. This is perhaps the reason why Vishishṭād-vaita became so popular as a religion of the destitute and the helpless; it is the religion of one who had nothing to offer to his Master except the whole of his soul. Little wonder, then, that it permeated the entire fabric of the whole Hindu society and left an indelible impression upon it. This ethical religion of heart is perhaps a more lasting contribution of Rāmānuja than his philosophical speculation.

As for Shankara, for Rāmānuja too perfection consists in attaining a state of freedom from mundane existence. This is, however, only a negative interpretation. Positively, it signifies much more than this. The freedom attained here is but a means to the attainment of a supra-mundane mode of existence wherein the freed soul enjoys the highest bliss in the presence of God. Another equally unique feature of the Vishishṭādvaita philosopher's world-view is the belief that such a soul, on discarding the mortal frame of the body at death, receives in the kingdom of God another body made of the immortal stuff, called shuddhasattva. It is by means of this body that the liberated soul enjoys the blissful company of its supreme Master in heaven (vaikuṇṭha). Some very fascinating descriptions are given of this region of the blessed. There God, affectionately called Hari, Nārāyaṇa, Shrī, Ishvara, and so on, is seated on his white throne, accompanied by his consort, Lakshmī, and all the time surrounded by the liberated souls who are all in deep spiritual intercourse with one another and express the same sentiments of love and reverence for their Master. It is a place where there reigns eternal peace and freedom. Each liberated soul seeks its joy and happiness in following the will of his supreme Master. When a human soul (jīva) finally succeeds in cutting asunder the knots of bondage it qualifies itself for an eternal abode in the kingdom of the blessed. There it is accorded a hearty welcome by the liberated souls and ushered in the presence of the Lord who affectionately admits it into his divine order. Like all others, he also shares eternal communion with Nārāyaṇa and takes special pride in following his will. It has a direct vision of the infinite attributes and glories of God, and rejoices in singing in praise for them. He derives his special pleasure in the calm contemplation of these attributes. One striking point which clearly emerges in this exposition is that for our philosopher there is no such state as jīvan-mukti. One attains perfection and freedom only when one assumes a fine body in the kingdom of God and leads an embodied existence for all eternity. Though embodied, the liberated soul is not affected by any change as implied in mortality. There the soul leads an existence full of eternal bliss and self-sufficiency. It is the state where there is neither suffering nor want.

The Upanishadic contribution

If what has been stated before is any indication, the metaphysics propounded by the Upanishads is a challenge even to the modern mind. The profundity and subtlety so clearly evidenced in their attempt to build up a case for spiritual absolutism are remarkable. This absolutism is unique not only in the history of Indian philosophy but also in the entire human thought. The Upanishadic philosophy is expressive of the concern and commitment of the ancient Indians in their quest for the truth. Most subsequent Indian thinkers did feel its impact, though each sought to find his own explanation. That is precisely why Indian philosophy assumed different roles at the hands of different philosophers, but only within the general framework provided by the Upanishads.

Buddha was indeed the first Indian thinker to give a new dimension to the Upanishadic thought by beginning not with the indescribable self but with all that constitutes the realm of the not-self. If the self, according to the Upanishads, is indefinable (neti, neti), why not, said Buddha, begin with the not-self? This was indeed the first attempt of its kind made by Buddha and, happily enough, he was successful in this. He undertook a penetrative analysis of the realm of the not-self and sought to show thereby that an ultimate state of bliss was possible of attainment through a strictly moral code. That

explains S. Radhakrishnan's remark that the teaching of Buddha is a restatement of the teaching of the
Upanishads.[4]

The Mahāyānists' attempt to reduce the world
of experience to the relativity of thought is a lauda-
ble one and points to the same direction. As we
have noted before, the Mahāyānists undertook a
thorough probe into the activity of thought and
sought to show that all conceptual categories could
only reveal a world that was relative and conditioned. The real, they argued, was unconditioned and
absolute, and could not be accessible to thought-
activity. The real, in their view, was of the nature
of pure consciousness (prajnā-pāramitā) and the ultimate goal was no other than the realization of one's
self as this consciousness. On the attainment of this
goal the whole world melts away into nothingness.
What appears to be the world in ordinary experience gives way to spiritual vision whereupon one
discovers one's self as of the very essence of absolute
consciousness. Evidently, the Mahāyānists' attempt
was to vindicate the Upanishadic thought by means
of the application of the dialectic method. This
method was certainly the outcome of a strictly logical
approach to the problem of reality. It would, then,
appear that this was a new approach to the old
Upanishadic conception of reality. In this respect
the Mahāyānists have no parallel in the entire history of the development of the Indian tradition in
philosophy.

The Jainas, too, approach the Upanishadic
problem from a new perspective and sought to show

that all the familiar categories of Being and Non-being, with all their possible combinations and permutations, were relative to the world of thought-activity alone, and could not, therefore, give us the true knowledge of the ultimate reality. Here, too, the results were almost the same. The aim, in their view, was the attainment of self as in essence all-powerful, all-blissful. This is the highest state one can attain as the *summum bonum*. Such a state is characteristic of absolute knowledge (kevala-jñāna) whereupon all distinctions relative to the phenomenal world disappear.

Shankara was perhaps the most consistent exponent of the Vedānta philosophy of the Upanishads. He wrote elaborate commentaries on the various Upanishads and sought to show that what alone could be ultimately real was only the Self. He sought to perfect the Upanishadic methodology in the light of his own reasoning and thereby proceeded to show that the familiar categories of Being and Non-being could not take us anywhere to the ultimate truth. They could well explain the ordinary world of experience, but they could not take us beyond it, since they were all found to be vitiated by self-contradiction. The conclusion he sought to establish was that Brahman was indefinable (anirvachanīya).

It is now abundantly clear that the three chief traditions of Indian philosophy—the Upanishads and Shankara's Advaita-Vedānta, Jainism, and Buddhism—had the common aim, namely, to devise and develop a method of philosophical investigations and arrive at the notion of an ultimate reality in the light thereof. But it will have to be granted that the Upanishads were the pioneers in setting the tone of these subsequent traditions.[5] Each of these traditions was free to develop its own methodology and deduce its own conclusions. And this is a positive proof of the fact that the subsequent traditions could not shake themselves wholly free from the Upanishadic line of reasoning.

Refcrances

1. D.T. Suzuki, *Outlines of Mahāyāna Buddhism*, pp. 293-94.
2. This is an expression of the Upanishadic view that Brahman is real, knowledge and infinite (satyam, jnañam, anantam).
3. See *Shri-bhāshya*, I.i.1.
4. *Indian Philosophy*, Vol. I, pp. 470,471.
5. See my book, *The Philosophy of Truth: The Indian Quest for Reality*, Chapters I, II and III.